I0650740

CIVIL WAR SPEECHES:
THE NORTH

Maureen Harrison & Steve Gilbert, Editors

Excellent Books
Carlsbad, California

EXCELLENT BOOKS
Suite 108A-204
300 Carlsbad Village Drive
Carlsbad, CA 92008-2999

Publisher's Cataloging in Publication Data

Civil War Speeches: The North/
  Maureen Harrison, Steve Gilbert, editors.
    p. cm.
Bibliography: p.

United States–History–Civil War, 1861–1865, Oratory. I. Title.
II. Harrison, Maureen. III. Gilbert, Steve.
E487. C5855 2011 LC 2008908017
973.713 -dc 21.
ISBN 978-1-880780-32-9

INTRODUCTION

No television, no internet, no twitter. 150 years ago public opinion was shaped, not by 30-second sound bytes, banner ads, or 140-character messages. It was shaped by people climbing upon the stage and speaking persuasively to audiences large and small. One speech, carefully constructed, passionately given, and widely circulated, could and did turn obscure politicians into national figures.

Civil War Speeches is a collection of passionate words spoken by the people most intimately involved in the great debates of their time.

There is an unmistakable truth that one man's traitorous zealot is another man's passionate patriot. The difference is geography. To Southerners, Frederick Douglass and William Garrison, proponents of the abolition of slavery, were extremists threatening a cherished way of life. To Northerners, firebrands like William Loundes Yancy and Robert Barnwell Rhett were fanatics seeking to destroy the union of the states.

Their war of words soon devolved into the bloodiest war in American history. These volumes chronicle the drama that was played out over the 15-year period (1850-1865) leading up to and comprising the Civil War. Read chronologically, these speeches show the evolution of public sentiment, molded by the speakers that placed great masses on a collision course.

There are no glorious, death-defying bayonet charges to be found in these volumes. The weapons used by the speakers were simple appeals to patriotism and the defense of home and hearth; it was a question of whose flag was to fly over whose country.

Civil War Speeches is designed to be every reader's speech reference and every librarian's resource. The editors have made every effort to either obtain the original text, or to reconcile differing texts, to provide the reader the authentic words of the speakers. The only change we have made to the text is to carefully edit the essential sections presented into modern spelling and grammar.

Civil War Speeches presents 37 important speeches (20 in the North's volume, 17 in the South's volume) each placed in its correct historic context by a biographical sketch of the speaker, a history of the speech, and a thorough bibliography. Edited for readers, writers, and researchers at all levels, *Civil War Speeches* provides the user with a right-at-the fingertips, easy-to-access speech reference.

A century and a half after the guns have fallen silent, and long after the speakers have gone to their graves, their words still have power to stir the American soul, North and South.

—M.H. & S.G.

TABLE OF SPEECHES

Abraham Lincoln
A House Divided Against Itself
62

A house divided against itself cannot stand. I believe this government cannot endure, permanently half slave and half free.

—June 16, 1858

Stephen Douglas
Popular Sovereignty
72

I do not regard the Negro as my equal, and positively deny that he is my other or any kin to me whatever.

—August 21, 1858

William Seward
The Irrepressible Conflict
82

It is an irrepressible conflict between opposing and enduring forces, and it means that the United States must and will, sooner or later, become either entirely a slave-holding nation or entirely a free-labor nation.

—October 25, 1858

John Brown
On The Gallows
88

I did no wrong, but right. Now, if it is deemed necessary that I forfeit my life ... I say, let it be done.

—November 2, 1859

Andrew Johnson
Not a Southern Or Any Other Confederacy
91

I would rather see this Government today converted into a consolidated government. It would be better ... than breaking up this splendid, this magnificent, this stupendous fabric of human government, the most perfect that the world ever saw, and which has succeeded thus far without a parallel in the history of the world.

—December 18, 1860

William Tecumseh Sherman
War Is A Terrible Thing!
96

You people of the South don't know what you are doing. This country will be drenched in blood, and God only knows how it will end. It is all folly, madness, a crime against civilization!

—December 24, 1860

Abraham Lincoln
First Inaugural Address
99

The mystic chords of memory, stretching from every battle-field, and patriot grave, to every living heart and hearth-stone, all over this broad land, will yet swell the chorus of the Union, when again touched, as surely they will be, by the better angels of our nature.

—March 4, 1861

Angelina Grimke Weld
My Country Is Bleeding
110

Abolitionists never sought place or power. All they asked was freedom; all they wanted was that the white man should take his foot off the Negro's neck.

—May 14, 1863

Sojourner Truth
The Great Sin of Prejudice Against Color
115

[Get] rid of your prejudice, and learn to love colored children that you may be all the children of your Father who is in Heaven.

—June 12, 1863

Henry Ward Beecher
Slavery
117

Slavery is the cause of the war. Slavery has been working for more than one hundred years, and a chronic evil cannot be suddenly cured; and as war is the remedy, you must be patient to have the conflict long enough to cure the inveterate hereditary sore.

—October 16, 1863

Abraham Lincoln
The Gettysburg Address
131

We here highly resolve that these dead shall not have died in vain—that this nation, under God, shall have a new birth of freedom—and that government of the people, by the people, for the people, shall not perish from the earth.

—November 19, 1863

Frederick Douglass
What The Black Man Wants
133

No class of men can, without insulting their own nature, be content with any deprivation of their rights.

—January 26, 1865

Abraham Lincoln
Second Inaugural Address
142

With malice toward none, with charity for all, with firmness in the right, as God gives us to see the right—let us strive on to finish the work we are in.

—March 4, 1865

Andrew Johnson
Treason Must Be Made Odious
145

Treason must be made odious; that traitors must be impoverished, their social power broken though; they must be made to feel the penalty of their crime.

—April 4, 1865

Ralph Waldo Emerson
The Death of Abraham Lincoln
150

There, by his courage, his justice, his even temper, his fertile counsel, his humanity, he stood, an heroic figure in the centre of an heroic epoch. He is the true history of the American people in his time.

April 19, 1865

William Henry Seward
Higher Law
March 11, 1850

William Henry Seward, one of the great anti-slavery speakers, was born on May 16, 1801 in Florida, New York. He attended Schenectady, New York's Union College and began to practice law in 1822. He served as a New York State Senator, as Governor of New York, and, in 1849, as a U.S. Senator. His speech on Higher Law, *delivered during the Senate debate of Henry Clay's* Compromise of 1850, *established him as an anti-slavery spokesman.*

.... [Assuming] the same premises, to wit, that all men are equal by the law of nature and of nations, the right of property in slaves falls to the ground; for one who is equal to another cannot be the owner or property of that other. But you answer, that the Constitution recognizes property in slaves. It would be sufficient, then, to reply, that this constitutional recognition must be void, because it is repugnant to the law of nature and of nations. But I deny that the Constitution recognizes property in man. I submit, on the other hand, most respectfully, that the Constitution not merely does not affirm that principle, but, on the contrary, altogether excludes it.

The Constitution does not expressly affirm anything on the subject; all that it contains is two incidental allusions to slaves. These are, first, in the provision establishing a ratio of representation and taxation; and secondly, in the provision relating to fugitives from labor. In both cases, the Constitution designedly mentions slaves, not as slaves, much less as chattels, but as persons. That this recognition of them as persons was designed is historically known, and I think was never denied....

I deem it established, then, that the Constitution does not recognize property in man, but leaves that question, as between the states, to the law of nature and of nations. That law ... is founded on the reason of things. When God had created the earth, with its

1

wonderful adaptations, He gave dominion over it to man, absolute human dominion. The title of that dominion, thus bestowed, would have been incomplete, if the lord of all terrestrial things could himself have been the property of his fellowman.

The right to have a slave implies the right in some one to make the slave; that right must be equal and mutual, and this would resolve society into a state of perpetual war. But if we grant the original equality of the states, and grant also the constitutional recognition of slaves as property, still the argument we are considering fails. Because the states are not parties to the Constitution as states; it is the Constitution of the people of the United States.

But even if the states continue under the constitution as states, they nevertheless surrendered their equality as states, and submitted themselves to the sway of the numerical majority, with qualifications or checks; first, of the representation of three-fifths of slaves in the ratio of representation and taxation; and, secondly, of the equal representation of states in the Senate.

The proposition of an established classification of states as slave states and free states, as insisted on by some, and into northern and southern, as maintained by others, seems to me purely imaginary, and of course the supposed equilibrium of those classes a mere conceit.... [The] Constitution was made not only for southern and northern states, but for states neither northern nor southern, namely, the western states, their coming in being foreseen and provided for.

.... The United States are a political state, or organized society, whose end is government, for the security, welfare, and happiness of all who live under its protection. The theory I am combating reduces the objects of government to the mere spoils of conquest. Contrary to a theory so debasing, the preamble of the Constitution not only asserts the sovereignty to be, not in the states, but in the people, but also promulgates the objects of the Constitution: *We, the people of the United States, in order to form a more perfect union, establish justice, insure domestic tranquility, provide for the* common defense, *promote the General Welfare, and secure the* blessings of liberty, *do ordain and establish this Constitution.*

Objects sublime and benevolent! They exclude the very idea of conquests, to be either divided among states or even enjoyed by them, for the purpose of securing, not the blessings of liberty, but the evils of slavery. There is a novelty in the principle of the proposed compromise which condemns it. Simultaneously with the establishment of the Constitution, Virginia ceded to the United States her domain, which then extended to the Mississippi, and was even claimed to extend to the Pacific Ocean. Congress accepted it, and unanimously devoted the domain to freedom, in the language from which the ordinance now so severely condemned was borrowed. Five states have already been organized on this domain, from all of which, in pursuance of that ordinance, slavery is excluded. How did it happen that this theory of the equality of states, of the classification of states, of the equilibrium of states, of the title of the states, to common enjoyment of the domain, or to an equitable and just partition between them, was never promulgated, nor even dreamed of, by the slave states, when they unanimously consented to that ordinance?

There is another aspect of the principle of compromise which deserves consideration. It assumes that slavery, if not the only institution in a slave state, is at least a ruling institution, and that this characteristic is recognized by the Constitution. But slavery is only *one* of many institutions there. Freedom is equally an institution there. Slavery is only a temporary, accidental, partial, and incongruous one. Freedom on the contrary, is a perpetual, organic, universal one, in harmony with the Constitution of the United States. The slaveholder himself stands under the protection of the latter, in common with all the free citizens of the state. But it is, moreover, an indispensable institution. You may separate slavery from South Carolina, and the state will still remain; but if you subvert freedom there, the state will cease to exist....

It is true, indeed, that the national domain is ours. It is true it was acquired by the valor and with the wealth of the whole nation. But we hold, nevertheless, no arbitrary power over it. We hold no arbitrary authority over anything, whether acquired lawfully or seized by usurpation. The Congress regulates our stewardship; the Constitution devotes the domain to union, to justice, to defense, to welfare, and to liberty.

But there is a higher law than the Constitution, which regulates our authority over the domain, and devotes it to the same noble purposes. The territory is a part, no inconsiderable part, of the common heritage of mankind, bestowed upon them by the Creator of the universe. We are his stewards, and must so discharge our trust as to secure in the highest attainable degree their happiness....

This is a state, and we are deliberating for it, just as our fathers deliberated in establishing the institutions we enjoy. Whatever superiority there is in our condition and hopes of those over any other "kingdom" or "estate," is due to the fortunate circumstance that our ancestors did not leave things to "take their chance," but that they "added amplitude and greatness" to our commonwealth "by introducing such ordinances, constitutions, and customs, as were wise." We in our term have succeeded to the same responsibilities, and we cannot approach the duty before us wisely or justly, except we raise ourselves to the great consideration of how we can most certainly "sow greatness to our posterity and successors."

And now the simple, bold, and even awful question which presents itself to us is this: Shall we, who are founding institutions, social and political, for countless millions; shall we, who know by experience the wise and the just, and are free to choose them, and to reject the erroneous and the unjust; shall we establish human bondage, or permit it by our sufferance to be established? Sir, our forefathers would not have hesitated an hour. They found slavery existing here, and they left it only because they could not remove it. There is not only no free state which would now establish it, but there is no slave state, which, if it had had the free alternative as we now have, would have founded slavery. Indeed, our revolutionary predecessors had precisely the same question before them in establishing an organic law under which the states of Ohio, Indiana, Michigan, Illinois, and Wisconsin, have since come into the Union, and they solemnly repudiated and excluded slavery from those states forever. I confess that the most alarming evidence of our degeneracy which has yet been given is found in the fact that we even debate such a question.

... [There] is no Christian nation, thus free to choose as we are, which would establish slavery. I speak on due consideration because Britain, France, and Mexico, have abolished slavery, and all other European states are preparing to abolish it as speedily as they can. We cannot establish slavery, because there are certain elements of the security, welfare, and greatness of nations, which we all admit, or ought to admit, and recognize as essential; and these are the security of natural rights, the diffusion of knowledge, and the freedom of industry. Slavery is incompatible with all of these; and, just in proportion to the extent that it prevails and controls in any republican state, just to that extent it subverts the principle of democracy, and converts the state into an aristocracy or a despotism....

Of all slavery, African slavery is the worst, for it combines practically the features of what is distinguished as real slavery or serfdom with the personal slavery known in the oriental world. Its domestic features lead to vice, while its political features render it injurious and dangerous to the state.

I cannot stop to debate long with those who maintain that slavery itself is practically economical and humane. I might be content with saying that there are some axioms in political science that a statesman or a founder of states may adopt, especially in the Congress of the United States, and that among those axioms are these: That all men are created equal, and have inalienable rights of life, liberty, and the choice of pursuits of happiness; that knowledge promotes virtue, and righteousness exalteth a nation; that freedom is preferable to slavery, and that democratic governments, where they can be maintained by acquiescence, without force, are preferable to institutions exercising arbitrary and irresponsible power.

It remains only to remark that our own experience has proved the dangerous influence and tendency of slavery. All our apprehensions of dangers, present and future, begin and end with slavery. If slavery, limited as it yet is, now threatens to subvert the Constitution, how can we as wise and prudent statesmen, enlarge its boundaries and increase its influence, and thus increase already impending dangers? Whether, then, I regard merely the welfare of the future inhabitants of the new territories, or the security and welfare of the whole people of the United States, or the welfare of the whole family of mankind, I cannot consent to introduce slavery into any part of this continent which is now exempt from what seems to me so great an evil. These are my reasons for declining to compromise the question relating to slavery as a condition of the admission of California.

.... Congress *may* admit new states; and since Congress may admit, it follows that Congress may *reject* new states. The discretion of Congress in admitting is absolute, except that, when admitted, the state must be a republican state, and must be a state, that is, it shall have the constitutional form and powers of a state. But the greater includes the less, and therefore Congress may impose *conditions* of admission not inconsistent with those fundamental powers and forms. Boundaries are such. The reservation of the public domain is such. The ordinance excluding slavery is such a condition. The organization of a territory is ancillary or preliminary; it is the inchoate, the initiative act of admission, and is performed under the clause granting the powers necessary to execute the express powers of the Constitution.

.... And the right to regulate property, to administer justice in regard to property, is assumed in every territorial charter. If we have the power to legislate concerning property, we have the power to legislate concerning personal rights. Freedom is a personal right; and Congress, being the supreme legislature, has the same right in regard to property and personal rights in territories that the states would have if organized.

The next of this class of arguments is, that the inhibition of slavery in the new territories is unnecessary; and when I come to

6

this question, I encounter the loss of many who lead in favor of admitting California....

The argument is, that the Proviso is unnecessary. I answer, then there can be no error in insisting upon it. But why is it unnecessary? It is said, first, by reason of climate. I answer, if this be so, why do not the representatives of the slave states concede the Proviso? They deny that the climate prevents the introduction of slavery. Then I will leave nothing to a contingency. But, in truth, I think the weight of the argument is against the proposition. Is there any climate where slavery has not existed? It has prevailed all over Europe, from sunny Italy to bleak England, and is existing now, stronger than in any other land, in ice-bound Russia. But it will be replied, that this is not African slavery. I rejoin, that only makes the case stronger. If this vigorous Saxon race of ours was reduced to slavery while it retained the courage of semi-barbarism in its own high northern latitude, what security does climate afford against the transplantation of the more gentle, more docile, and already enslaved and debased African to the genial climate of New Mexico and Eastern California?

... [There] is no climate uncongenial to slavery. It is true it is less productive than free labor in many northern countries. But so it is less productive than free white labor in even tropical climates. Labor is in quick demand in all new countries. Slave labor is cheaper than free labor, and it would go first into new regions; and wherever it goes it brings labor into dishonor, and therefore free white labor avoids competition with it.... I might rely on climate if I had not been born in a land where slavery existed—and this land was all of it north of the fortieth parallel of latitude; and if I did not know the struggle it has cost, and which is yet going on, to get complete relief from the institution and its baleful consequences. I desire to propound this question to those who are now in favor of dispensing with the Wilmot Proviso: Was the ordinance of 1787 necessary or not? Necessary, we all agree. It has received too many elaborate eulogiums to be now decried as an idle and superfluous thing. And yet that ordinance extended the inhibition of slavery from the thirty-seventh to the fortieth parallel of north latitude. And now we are told that the inhibition named is unnecessary anywhere north of 36° 30'! We are told that we may rely upon the laws of God, which prohibit slave labor north of that line, and that it is absurd to re-enact the laws of God.... [There] is no human enactment which is just that is not a re-enactment of the law of God. The Constitution of the United States and the constitutions of all the states are full of such re-enactments. Wherever I find a law of God or a law of nature disregarded, or in danger of being disregarded, there I shall vote to reaffirm it, with all the sanction of the civil authority. But I find no authority for the position that climate prevents slavery anywhere. It is the indolence of mankind in any climate, and not any natural necessity, that introduces slavery in any climate.

.... Slavery has never obtained anywhere by express legislative authority, but always by trampling down laws higher than any mere municipal laws—the laws of nature and of nations. There can be no oppression in superadding the sanction of Congress to the authority which is so weak and so vehemently questioned. And there is some possibility, if not probability, that the institution may obtain a foothold surreptitiously, if it shall not be absolutely forbidden by our own authority.

What is insisted upon, therefore, is not a mere abstraction or a mere sentiment, as is contended by those who waive the proviso. And what is conclusive on the subject is, that it is conceded on all hands that the effect of insisting on it is to prevent the intrusion of slavery into the region to which it is proposed to apply it.

It is insisted that the diffusion of slavery will not increase its evils. The argument seems to me merely specious, and quite unsound.... Is slavery stronger or weaker in these United States, from its diffusion into Missouri? Is slavery weaker or stronger in these United States, from the exclusion of it from the northwest territory? The answers to these questions will settle the whole controversy.

And this brings me to the great and all-absorbing argument that the Union is in danger of being dissolved, and that it can only be saved by compromise. I do not know what I would not do to save the Union; and therefore I shall bestow upon this subject a very deliberate consideration.

I do not overlook the fact that the entire delegation from the slave states, although they differ in regard to the details of the compromise proposed, and perhaps in regard to the exact circumstances of the crisis, seem to concur in this momentous warning. Nor do I doubt at all the patriotic devotion to the Union which is expressed by those from whom this warning proceeds. And yet, ... although such warnings have been uttered with impassioned solemnity in my hearing every day for near three months, my confidence in the Union remains unshaken....

[In] my humble judgment, it is not the fierce conflict of parties that we are seeing and hearing; but, on the contrary, it is the agony of distracted parties—a convulsion resulting from the too narrow foundations of both the great parties, and of all parties—foundations laid in compromises of natural justice and of human liberty. A question, a moral question, transcending the too narrow creeds of parties, has arisen; the public conscience expands with it, and the green withes of party associations give way and break, and fall off from it. No, sir; it is not the state that is dying of the fever of party spirit. It is merely a paralysis of parties, premonitory however of their restoration, with new elements of health and vigor to be imbibed from that spirit of the age which is so justly called Progress.

Nor is the evil that of unlicensed, irregular, and turbulent faction. We are told that twenty legislatures are in session, burning like furnaces, heating and inflaming the popular passions. But these twenty legislatures are constitutional furnaces. They are performing their customary functions, imparting healthful heat and vitality while within their constitutional jurisdiction. If they rage beyond its limits, the popular passions of this country are not at all, I think, in danger of being inflamed to excess. No, sir; let none of these fires be extinguished. Forever let them burn and blaze. They are neither ominous meteors nor baleful comets, but planets; and bright and intense as their heat may be, it is their native temperature, and they must still obey the law which, by attraction to this solar center, holds them in their spheres.

I see nothing of that conflict between the southern and northern states, or between their representative bodies, which seems to be on all sides of me assumed. Not a word of menace, not a word of anger, not an intemperate word, has been uttered in the northern legislatures. They firmly but calmly assert their convictions; but at the same time they assert their unqualified consent to submit to the common arbiter, and for weal or woe abide the fortunes of the Union.

What if there be less of moderation in the legislatures of the south? It only indicates on which side the balance is inclining, and that the decision of the momentous question is near at hand. I agree with those who say there can be no peaceful dissolution— no dissolution of the Union by the secession of states; but that disunion, dissolution, happen when it may, will and must be revolution. I discover no omens of revolution. The predictions of the political astrologers do not agree as to the time or manner in which it is to occur....

What are the omens to which our attention is directed? I see nothing but a broad difference of opinion here, and the excitement consequent upon it.

I have observed that revolutions which begin in the palace seldom go beyond the palace walls, and they affect only the dynasty which reigns there. This revolution, if I understand it, began in this Senate chamber a year ago, when the representatives from the southern states assembled here and addressed their constituents on what were called the aggressions of the northern states. No revolution was designed at that time, and all that has happened since is the return to Congress of legislative resolutions, which seem to me to be only conventional responses to the address which emanated from the capitol.

... [In] any condition of society there can be no revolution without a cause, an adequate cause. What cause exists here? We are admitting a new state; but there is nothing new in that: we have already admitted seventeen before. But it is said that the slave states are in danger of losing political power by the admission of the new state. Well, sir, is there anything new in that? The slave states have always been losing political power, and they always will be while they have any to lose. At first, twelve of the thirteen states were slave states; now only fifteen out of thirty are slave states. Moreover, the change is constitutionally made, and the government was constructed so as to permit changes of the balance of power, in obedience to changes of the forces of the body politic....

[Those] who would alarm us with the terrors of revolution have not well considered the structure of this government, and the organization of its forces. It is a democracy of property and persons, with a fair approximation towards universal education, and operating by means of universal suffrage. The constituent members of this democracy are the only persons who could subvert it; and they are not the citizens of a metropolis like Paris, or of a region subjected to the influences of a metropolis like France; but they are husbandmen, dispersed over this broad land, on the mountain and on the plain, and on the prairie, from the ocean to the Rocky Mountains, and from the great lakes to the gulf; and this people are now, while we are discussing their imaginary danger, at peace and in their happy homes, as unconcerned and uninformed of their peril as they are of events occurring in the moon. Nor have the alarmists made due allowance in their calculations for the influence of conservative reaction, strong in any government, and irresistible in a rural republic, operating by universal suffrage. That principle of reaction is due to the force of the habits of acquiescence and loyalty among the people.... Do the alarmists remember that this government has stood sixty years already without exacting one drop of blood?—that this government has stood sixty years, and yet treason is an obsolete crime? That day, I trust, is far off when the fountains of popular contentment shall be broken up; but whenever it shall come, it will bring forth a higher illustration than has ever yet been given of the excellence of the democratic system; for then it will be seen how calmly, how firmly, how nobly, a great people can act in preserving their Constitution; whom "love of country moveth, example teacheth, company comforteth, emulation quickeneth, and glory exalteth."

When the founders of the new republic of the south come to draw over the face of this empire, along or between its parallels of latitude or longitude, their ominous lines of dismemberment, soon to be broadly and deeply shaded with fraternal blood, they may come to the discovery then, if not before, that the natural and even political connections of the region embraced forbid such a partition; that its possible divisions are not northern and southern at all, but eastern and western, Atlantic and Pacific; and that nature and commerce have allied indissolubly for weal and woe the seceders and those from whom they are to be separated; that while they would rush into a civil war to restore an imaginary equilibrium between the northern states and the southern states, a new equilibrium has taken its place, in which all those states are on one side, and the boundless west is on the other.

... [When] the founders of the republic of the south come to draw those fearful lines, they will indicate what portions of the continent are to be broken off with their connection from the Atlantic, through the St. Lawrence, the Hudson, the Delaware, the Potomac, and the Mississippi; what portion of this people are to be denied the use of the lakes, the railroads, and the canals, now constituting common and customary avenues of travel, trade, and social intercourse; what families and kindred are to be separated, and converted into enemies; and what states are to be the scenes of perpetual border warfare, aggravated by interminable horrors of servile insurrection? When those portentous lines shall be drawn, they will disclose what portion of this people is to retain the army and the navy, and the flag of so many victories; and on the other hand, what portion of the people is to be subjected to new and onerous imposts, direct taxes, and forced loans, and conscriptions, to maintain an opposing army, an opposing navy, and the new and hateful banner of sedition. Then the projectors of the new republic of the south will meet the question—and they may well prepare now to answer it—What is all this for?

12

What intolerable wrong, what unfraternal injustice, have rendered these calamities unavoidable? What gain will this unnatural revolution bring to us? The answer will be: All this is done to secure the institution of African slavery.

And then, if not before, the question will be discussed, What is this institution of slavery, that it should cause these unparalleled sacrifices and these disastrous afflictions? And this will be the answer: When the Spaniards, few in number, discovered the western Indies and adjacent continental America, they needed labor to draw forth from its virgin stores some speedy return to the cupidity of the court and the bankers of Madrid. They enslaved the indolent, inoffensive, and confiding natives, who perished by thousands, and even by millions, under that new and unnatural bondage. A humane ecclesiastic advised the substitution of Africans reduced to captivity in their native wars, and a pious princess adopted the suggestion, with a dispensation from the head of the church, granted on the ground of the prescriptive right of the Christian to enslave the heathen, to effect his conversion. The colonists of North America, innocent in their unconsciousness of wrong, encouraged the slave traffic, and thus the labor of subduing their territory devolved chiefly upon the African race. A happy conjuncture brought on an awakening of the conscience of mankind to the injustice of slavery, simultaneously with the independence of the colonies. Massachusetts, Connecticut, Rhode Island, New Hampshire, Vermont, New York, New Jersey, and Pennsylvania, welcomed and embraced the spirit of universal emancipation. Renouncing luxury, they secured influence and empire. But the states of the south, misled by a new and profitable culture, elected to maintain and perpetuate slavery; and thus, choosing luxury, they lost power and empire.

When this answer shall be given, it will appear that the question of dissolving the Union is a complex question; that it embraces the fearful issue whether the Union shall stand, and slavery, under the steady, peaceful action of moral, social, and political causes, be removed by gradual voluntary effort, and with compensation, or whether the Union shall be dissolved, and civil wars ensue,

13

bringing on violent but complete and immediate emancipation. We are now arrived at that stage of our national progress when that crisis can be foreseen, when we must foresee it. It is directly before us. Its shadow is upon us. It darkens the legislative halls, the temples of worship, and the home and the hearth. Every question, political, civil, or ecclesiastical, however foreign to the subject of slavery, brings up slavery as an incident, and the incident supplants the principle question. We hear of nothing but slavery, and we can talk of nothing but slavery. And now, it seems to me that all our difficulties, embarrassments, and dangers, arise, not out of unlawful perversions of the question of slavery, as some suppose, but from the want of moral courage to meet this question of emancipation as we ought. Consequently, we hear on one side demands—absurd, indeed, but yet unceasing—for an immediate and unconditional abolition of slavery—as if any power, except the people of the slave states, could abolish it, and as if they could be moved to abolish it by merely sounding the trumpet loudly and proclaiming emancipation, while the institution is interwoven with all their social and political interests, constitutions, and customs.

On the other hand, our statesmen say that "slavery has always existed, and, for aught they know or can do, it always must exist. God permitted it, and he alone can indicate the way to remove it." As if the Supreme Creator, after giving us the instructions of his providence and revelation for the illumination of our minds and consciences, did not leave us in all human transactions, with due invocations of his Holy Spirit, to seek out his will and execute it for ourselves.

.... I feel assured that slavery must give way, and will give way, to the salutary instructions of economy, and to the ripening influences of humanity; that emancipation is inevitable, and is near; that it may be hastened or hindered; and that whether it shall be peaceful or violent, depends upon the question whether it be hastened or hindered; that all measures which fortify slavery or extend it, tend to be the consummation of violence; all that check its extension and abate its strength, tend to its peaceful extirpa-

14

tion. But I will adopt none but lawful, constitutional, and peaceful means, to secure even that end; and none such can I or will I forego. Nor do I know any important or responsible political body that proposes to do more than this. No free state claims to extend its legislation into a slave state. None claims that Congress shall usurp power to abolish slavery in the slave states. None claims that any violent, unconstitutional, or unlawful measure shall be embraced. And, on the other hand, if we offer no scheme or plan for the adoption of the slave states, with the assent and cooperation of Congress, it is only because the slave states are unwilling as yet to receive such suggestions, or even to entertain the question of emancipation in any form.

.... I have thus endeavored to show that there is not now, and there is not likely to occur any adequate cause for revolution in regard to slavery. But you reply that, nevertheless, you must have guaranties; and the first one is for the surrender of fugitives from labor. That guaranty you cannot have, as I have already shown, because you cannot roll back the tide of social progress. You must be content with what you have. If you wage war against us, you can, at most, only conquer us, and then all you can get will be a treaty, and that you have already.

But you insist on a guaranty against the abolition of slavery in the District of Columbia, or war. Well, when you shall have declared war against us, what shall hinder us from immediately decreeing that slavery shall cease within the national capitol?

You say that you will not submit to the exclusion of slaves from the new territories. What will you gain by resistance? Liberty follows the sword, although her sway is one of peace and beneficence. Can you propagate slavery then by the sword?

You insist that you cannot submit to the freedom with which slavery is discussed in the free states. Will war—a war for slavery—arrest or even moderate that discussion? ... [That] discussion will not cease; war will only inflame it in to a greater height. It is part of the eternal conflict between truth and error— between mind and physical force—the conflict of man against the obstacles which oppose his way to an ultimate and glorious destiny. It will go on until you shall terminate it in the only way in which any state or nation has ever terminated it—by yielding to it—yielding in your own time, and in your own manner, indeed, but nevertheless yielding to the progress of emancipation. You will do this, sooner or later, whatever may be your opinion now; because nations which were prudent and humane, and wise as you are, have done so already.

... [The] slave states have no reason to fear that this inevitable change will go too far or too fast for their safety or welfare. It cannot well go too fast or too far, if the only alternative is a war of races.

.... So long as slavery shall possess the cotton-fields, the sugar-fields, and the rice-fields of the world, so long will commerce and capital yield it toleration and sympathy. Emancipation is a democratic revolution....

Slavery has a guaranty still stronger ... in the prejudices of caste and color, which induce even large majorities in all the free states to regard sympathy with the slave as an act of unmanly humiliation and self-abasement, although philosophy meekly expresses her distrust of the asserted natural superiority of the white race, and confidently denies that such a superiority, if justly claimed, could give a title to oppression.

There remains one more guaranty—one that has seldom failed you, and will seldom fail you hereafter. New states cling in closer alliance than older ones to the federal power. The concentration of the slave power enables you for long periods to control the federal government with the aid of new states. I do not know the sentiments of the representatives of California; but, my word for it, if they should be admitted on this floor today, against your most obstinate opposition, they would, on all questions really affecting your interests, be found at your side.

With these alliances to break the force of emancipation, there will be no disunion and no secession. I do not say that there may not be disturbance, though I do not apprehend even that.... The ma-

16

chinery of our system is necessarily complex. A pivot may drop out here, a lever may be displaced there, a wheel may fall out of gearing elsewhere, but the machinery will soon recover its regularity, and move on just as before, with even better adaptation and adjustment to overcome new obstructions.

There are many well-disposed persons who are alarmed at the occurrence of any such disturbance. The failure of a legislative body to organize is to their apprehension a fearful omen, and an extra-constitutional assemblage to consult upon public affairs is with them cause for desperation. Even senators speak of the Union as if it existed only by consent, and, as it seems to be implied, by the assent of the legislatures of the states. On the contrary, the union was not founded in voluntary choice, nor does it exist by voluntary consent.

A union was proposed to the colonies by Franklin and others, in 1754; but such was their aversion to an abridgment of their own importance, respectively, that it was rejected even under the pressure of a disastrous invasion by France.

A union of choice was proposed to the colonies in 1775; but so strong was their opposition, that they went through the war of independence without having established more than a mere council of consultation.

But with independence came enlarged interests of agriculture—absolutely new interests of manufactures—interests of commerce, of fisheries, of navigation, of a common domain, of common debts, of common revenues and taxation, of the administration of justice, of public defense, of public honor; in short, interests of common nationality and sovereignty—interests which at last compelled the adoption of a more perfect union—a National Government.

The genius, talents, and learning of Hamilton, of Jay, and of Madison, surpassing perhaps the intellectual power ever exerted before for the establishment of a government, combined with the serene but mighty influence of Washington, were only sufficient to secure the reluctant adoption of the Constitution that is now the object of all our affections and of the hopes of mankind. No wonder that the conflicts in which that Constitution was born, and the almost desponding solemnity of Washington, in his farewell address, impressed his countrymen and mankind with a profound distrust of its perpetuity! No wonder that while the murmurs of that day are yet ringing in our ears, we cherish that distrust, with pious reverence, as a national and patriotic sentiment!

But it is time to prevent the abuses of that sentiment. It is time to shake off that fear, for fear is always weakness. It is time to remember that government, even when it arises by chance or accident, and is administered capriciously or oppressively, is ever the strongest of all human institutions, surviving many social and ecclesiastical changes and convulsions; and that this Constitution of ours has all the inherent strength common to governments in general, and added to them has also the solidity and firmness derived from broader and deeper foundations in national justice, and a better civil adaptation to promote the welfare and happiness of mankind.

The Union, the creature of necessities, physical, moral, social, and political, endures by virtue of the same necessities; and these necessities are stronger than when it was produced....

The Union, then, is, not because merely that men choose that it shall be, but because some government must exist here, and no other government than this can. If it could be dashed to atoms by the whirlwind, the lightning, or the earthquake, today, it would rise again in all its just and magnificent proportions tomorrow. This nation is a globe, still accumulating upon accumulation, not a dissolving sphere.

I have heard somewhat here, and almost for the first time in my life, of divided allegiance—of allegiance to the south and to the Union—of allegiance to states severally and to the Union.... [If] sympathies with state emulation and pride of achievement could be allowed to raise up another sovereign to divide the allegiance of a citizen of the United States, I might recognize the claims of the state to which, by birth and gratitude, I belong—to the state of Hamilton and Jay, of Schuyler, of the Clintons, and of Fulton—the state which, with less than two hundred miles of natural navigation connected with the ocean, has, by her own enterprise, secured to herself the commerce of the continent, and is steadily advancing to command the commerce of the world. But for all this I know only one country and one sovereign—the United States of America and the American People. And such as my allegiance is, is the loyalty of every other citizen of the United States. As I speak, he will speak when his time arrives. He knows no other country and no other sovereign. He has life, liberty, property, and precious affections, and hopes for himself and for his posterity, treasured up in the ark of the Union. He knows as well and feels as strongly as I do, that this government is his own government; that he is a part of it; that it was established for him; and that it was maintained by him; that it is the only truly wise, just, free, and equal government, that has ever existed; that no other government could be so wise, just, free and equal; and that it is safer and more beneficent than any which time or change could bring into its place.

.... Let ... those who distrust the Union make compromises to save it. I shall not impeach their wisdom, as I certainly cannot their patriotism; but, indulging no such apprehensions myself, I shall vote for the admission of California directly, without conditions, without qualifications, and without compromise.

For the vindication of that vote, I look not to the verdict of the passing hour, disturbed as the public mind now is by conflicting interests and passions, but to that period, happily not far distant, when the vast regions over which we are now legislating shall have received their destined inhabitants.

While looking forward to that day, its countless generations seem to me to be rising up and passing in dim and shadowy review before us; and a voice comes forth from their serried ranks, saying:

"Waste your treasures and your armies, if you will; raze your fortifications to the ground; sink your navies into the sea; transmit to us even a dishonored name, if you must; but the soil you hold in trust for us—give it to us free. You found it free, and conquered it to extend a better and surer freedom over it. Whatever choice you have made for yourselves, let us have no partial freedom; let us all be free; let the reversion of your broad domain descend to us unencumbered, and free from the calamities and from the sorrows of human bondage."

Afterward

On October 25, 1858 in Rochester, New York, while campaigning for the 1860 Republican Presidential nomination, Seward delivered his second landmark anti-slavery speech, The Irrepressible Conflict, *which appears on page 82. While he lost the nomination to Abraham Lincoln, he served as U.S. Secretary of State in both the Lincoln and Johnson Cabinets. In 1867 he negotiated Seward's Treaty, the purchase of Alaska.*

William Seward died on October 10, 1872.

Selected Reading

Baker, George E., Editor. *The Works of William H. Seward.* New York, NY: AMS Press. 1972.

Denton, Lawrence M. *William Henry Seward and the Secession Crisis: The Effort to Prevent Civil War.* Jefferson, NC: McFarland. 2009.

Taylor, John M., *William Henry Seward: Lincoln's Right Hand,* New York, NY: HarperCollins. 1991.

Frederick Douglass
The Great Sin And Shame Of America
July 5, 1852

Born a slave on a Maryland plantation in 1817, Frederick Douglass escaped to the North on the Underground Railroad in 1838. He spoke powerfully against slavery on behalf of the American Anti-Slavery Society and became know as The Voice of the Colored People. *On July 5, 1854, in Rochester, New York's Corinthian Hall, Douglass delivered this landmark speech,* The Great Sin and Shame of America.

Fellow citizens, pardon me, and allow me to ask, why am I called upon to speak here today? What have I, or those I represent, to do with your national independence? Are the great principles of political freedom and of natural justice embodied in that Declaration of Independence extended to us? And am I, therefore, called upon to bring our humble offering to the national altar, and to confess the benefits, and express devout gratitude for the blessings, resulting from your independence to us?

Would to God, both for your sakes and ours, that an affirmative answer could be truthfully returned to these questions! Then would my task be light, and my burden easy and delightful. For who is there so cold that a nation's sympathy could not warm him? Who so obdurate and dead to the claims of gratitude that would not thankfully acknowledge such priceless benefits? Who so stolid and selfish that would not give his voice to swell the hallelujahs of a nation's jubilee, when the chains of servitude had been torn from his limbs? I am not that man. In a case like that, the dumb might eloquently speak, and the "lame man [leaps] as [a] hart."

But such is not the state of the case. I say it with a sad sense of the disparity between us. I am not included within the pale of this glorious anniversary! Your high independence only reveals the immeasurable distance between us. The blessings in which you this day rejoice are not enjoyed in common. The rich inheritance of justice, liberty, prosperity, and independence, bequeathed by your fathers, is shared by you, not by me. The sunlight that brought life and healing to you has brought stripes and death to me. This Fourth of July is yours, not mine. You may rejoice; I must mourn. To drag a man in fetters into the grand illuminated temple of liberty, and call upon him to join you in joyous anthems, were inhuman mockery and sacrilegious irony. Do you mean, citizens, to mock me, by asking me to speak today? If so, there is a parallel to your conduct. And let me warn you that it is dangerous to copy the example of a nation whose crimes, towering up to heaven, were thrown down by the breath of the Almighty, burying that nation in irrecoverable ruin! I can today take up the plaintive lament of a peeled and woe-smitten people.

> *By the rivers of Babylon, there we sat down. Yea! we wept when we remembered Zion. We hanged our harps upon the willows in the midst thereof. For there, they that carried us away captive, required of us a song; and they who wasted us required of us mirth, saying, "Sing us one of the songs of Zion." How can we sing the Lord's song in a strange land? If I forget thee, O Jerusalem, let my right hand forget her cunning. If I do not remember thee, let my tongue cleave to the roof of my mouth.*

Fellow citizens, above your national, tumultuous joy, I hear the mournful wail of millions, whose chains, heavy and grievous yesterday, are today rendered more intolerable by the jubilant shouts that reach them. If I do forget, if I do not faithfully remember those bleeding children of sorrow this day, *may my right hand forget her cunning, and may my tongue cleave to the roof of my mouth!* To forget them, to pass lightly over their wrongs, and to chime in with the popular theme, would be treason most scandalous and shocking, and would make me a reproach before God and the world. My subject, then, fellow-citizens, is American slavery. I shall see this day and its popular characteristics from the slave's point of view. Standing there, identified with the American bondman, making his wrongs mine, I do not hesitate to declare, with all my soul, that the character and conduct of this nation never looked blacker to me than on this Fourth of July. Whether we turn to the declarations of the past, or to the professions of the present, the conduct of the nation seems equally hideous and revolting. America is false to the past, false to the present, and solemnly binds herself to be false to the future. Standing with God and the crushed and bleeding slave on this occasion, I will, in the name of humanity which is outraged, in the name of liberty which is fettered, in the name of the Constitution and the Bible, which are disregarded and trampled upon, dare to call in question and to denounce, with all the emphasis I can command, everything that serves to perpetuate slavery—the great sin and shame of America! *I will not equivocate; I will not excuse*; I will use the severest language I can command; and yet not one word shall escape me that any man, whose judgment is not blinded by prejudice, or who is not at heart a slave-holder, shall not confess to be right and just.

But I fancy I hear someone of my audience say,

> *It is just in this circumstance that you and your brother abolitionists fail to make a favorable impression on the public mind. Would you argue more, and denounce less, would you persuade more and rebuke less, your cause would be much more likely to succeed.*

But, I submit, where all is plain, there is nothing to be argued. What point in the anti-slavery creed would you have me argue? On what branch of the subject do the people of this country need light? Must I undertake to prove that the slave is a man? That point is conceded already. Nobody doubts it. The slave-holders themselves acknowledge it in the enactment of laws for their government. They acknowledge it when they punish disobedience on the part of the slave. There are seventy-two crimes in the state of Virginia, which, if committed by a black man (no matter how ignorant he be), subject him to the punishment of death, while only two of these same crimes will subject a white man to the like punishment. What is this but the acknowledgment that the slave is a moral, intellectual, and responsible being? The manhood of the slave is conceded. It is admitted in the fact that Southern statute books are covered with enactments forbidding, under severe fines and penalties, the teaching of the slave to read or write. When you can point to any such laws, in reference to the beasts of the field, then I may consent to argue the manhood of the slave. When the dogs in your streets, when the fowls of the air, when the cattle on your hills, when the fish of the sea, and the reptiles that crawl, shall be unable to distinguish the slave from a brute, then will I argue with you that the slave is a man!

For the present, it is enough to affirm the equal manhood of the Negro race. Is it not astonishing that, while we are plowing, planting, and reaping, using all kinds of mechanical tools, erecting houses, constructing bridges, building ships, working in metals of brass, iron, copper, silver, and gold—that, while we are reading, writing, and ciphering, acting as clerks, merchants, and secretaries, having among us lawyers, doctors, ministers, poets, authors, editors, orators, and teachers—that, while we are engaged in all manner of enterprises common to other men—digging gold in California, capturing the whale in the Pacific, feeding sheep and cattle on the hillside, living, moving, acting, thinking, planning, living in families as husbands, wives, and children, and, above all, confessing and worshipping the Christian's God, and looking hopefully for life and immortality beyond the grave—we are called upon to prove that we are men!

Would you have me argue that man is entitled to liberty? That he is the rightful owner of his own body? You have already declared it. Must I argue the wrongfulness of slavery? Is that a question for Republicans? Is it to be settled by the rules of logic and argumentation, as a matter beset with great difficulty, involving a doubtful application of the principle of justice, hard to be understood? How should I look today in the presence of Americans, dividing and subdividing a discourse, to show that men have a natural right to freedom, speaking of it relatively and positively, negatively and affirmatively? To do so would be to make myself ridiculous and to offer an insult to your understanding. There is not a man beneath the canopy of heaven that does not know that slavery is wrong for him.

What? Am I to argue that it is wrong to make men brutes, to rob them of their liberty, to work them without wages, to keep them ignorant of their relations to their fellow-men, to beat them with

24

sticks, to flay their flesh with the lash, to load their limbs with irons, to hunt them with dogs, to sell them at auction, to sunder their families, to knock out their teeth, to burn their flesh, to starve them into obedience and submission to their masters? Must I argue that a system, thus marked with blood and stained with pollution, is wrong? No, I will not. I have better employment for my time and strength than such arguments would imply.

What, then, remains to be argued? Is it that slavery is not divine—that God did not establish it—that our doctors of divinity are mistaken? There is blasphemy in the thought. That which is inhuman cannot be divine. Who can reason on such a proposition? They that can, may; I cannot. The time for such argument is past.

At a time like this, scorching irony, not convincing argument, is needed. Oh! Had I the ability, and could I reach the nation's ear, I would today pour out a fiery stream of biting ridicule, blasting reproach, withering sarcasm, and stern rebuke. For it is not light that is needed, but fire—it is not the gentle shower, but thunder. We need the storm, the whirlwind, and the earthquake. The feeling of the nation must be quickened—the conscience of the nation must be roused—the propriety of the nation must be startled—the hypocrisy of the nation must be exposed—and its crimes against God and man must be proclaimed and denounced.

What to the American slave is your Fourth of July? I answer—a day that reveals to him, more than all other days in the year, the gross injustice and cruelty to which he is the constant victim. To him, your celebration is a sham—your boasted liberty, an unholy license—your national greatness, swelling vanity—your sounds of rejoicing are empty and heartless—your denunciations of tyrants, brass-fronted impudence—your shouts of liberty and equality, hollow mockery—your prayers and hymns, your sermons and thanksgivings, with all your religious parade and solemnity, are to him mere bombast, fraud, deception, impiety, and hypocrisy, a thin veil to cover up crimes which would disgrace a nation of savages. There is not a nation on the earth guilty of practices more shocking and bloody than are the people of these United States at this very hour.

Go where you may, search where you will, roam through all the monarchies and despotisms of the old world, travel through South America, search out every abuse, and when you have found the last, lay your facts by the side of the everyday practices of this nation, and you will say with me that, for revolting barbarity and shameless hypocrisy, America reigns without a rival.

Take the American slave trade which, we are told by the papers, is especially prosperous just now. Ex-senator Benton tells us that the price of men was never higher than now. He mentions the fact to show that slavery is in no danger. This trade is one of the peculiarities of American institutions. It is carried on in all the large towns and cities in one-half of this confederacy; and millions are pocketed every year by dealers in this horrid traffic. In several states this trade is a chief source of wealth. It is called (in contradistinction to the foreign slave trade) *the internal slave trade.* It is probably called so too in order to divert from it the horror with which the foreign slave trade is contemplated. That trade has long since been denounced by this government as piracy. It has been denounced with burning words, from the high places of the nation, as an execrable traffic. To arrest it, to put an end to it, this nation keeps a squadron, at immense cost, on the coast of Africa. Everywhere in this country, it is safe to speak of this foreign slave trade as a most inhuman traffic, opposed alike to the laws of God and of man. The duty to extirpate and destroy it is admitted even by our doctors of divinity. In order to put an end to it, some of these last have consented that their colored brethren (nominally free) should leave this country, and establish themselves on the western coast of Africa. It is, however, a notable fact that, while so much execration is poured out by Americans upon those engaged in the foreign slave trade, the men engaged in the slave trade between the states pass without condemnation, and their business is deemed honorable.

Behold the practical operation of this internal slave trade—the American slave trade sustained by American politics and Ameri-

26

can religion! Here you will see men and women reared like swine for the market. You know what is a swine-drover? I will show you a man-drover. They inhabit all our Southern states. They perambulate the country, and crowd the highways of the nation with droves of human stock. You will see one of these human flesh jobbers, armed with pistol, whip, and bowie knife, driving a company of a hundred men, women, and children, from the Potomac to the slave market at New Orleans. Those wretched people are to be sold singly, or in lots, to suit purchasers. They are food for the cotton field and the deadly sugar mill. Mark the sad procession as it moves wearily along, and the inhuman wretch who drives them. Hear his savage yells and his blood-chilling oaths, as he hurries on his affrighted captives. There, see the old man, with locks thinned and gray. Cast one glance, if you please, upon that young mother, whose shoulders are bare to the scorching sun, her briny tears falling on the brow of the babe in her arms. See, too, that girl of thirteen, weeping—yes, weeping—as she thinks of the mother from whom she has been torn. The drove moves tardily. Heat and sorrow have nearly consumed their strength. Suddenly you hear a quick snap, like the discharge of a rifle—the fetters clank, and the chain rattles simultaneously—your ears are saluted with a scream that seems to have torn its way to the center of your soul. The crack you heard was the sound of the slave whip; the scream you heard was from the woman you saw with the babe. Her speed had faltered under the weight of her child and her chains—that gash on her shoulder tells her to move on. Follow this drove to New Orleans. Attend the auction; see men examined like horses; see the forms of women rudely and brutally exposed to the shocking gaze of American slave-buyers. See this drove sold and separated forever; and never forget the deep, sad sobs that arose from that scattered multitude. Tell me, citizens, where, under the sun, can you witness a spectacle more fiendish and shocking? Yet this is but a glance at the American slave trade, as it exists at this moment, in the ruling part of the United States.

I was born amid such sights and scenes. To me the American slave trade is a terrible reality. When a child, my soul was often pierced with a sense of its horrors. I lived on Philpot Street, Fell's Point, Baltimore, and have watched from the wharves the slave ships in the basin, anchored from the shore, with their cargoes of human flesh, waiting for favorable winds to waft them down the Chesapeake. There was, at that time, a grand slave mart kept at the head of Pratt Street, by Austin Woldfolk. His agents were sent into every town and county in Maryland, announcing their arrival through the papers, and on flaming hand-bills headed, *Cash for Negroes*. These men were generally well dressed and very captivating in their manners, ever ready to drink, to treat, and to gamble. The fate of many a slave has depended upon the turn of a single card; and many a child has been snatched from the arms of its mother by bargains arranged in a state of brutal drunkenness.

The flesh-mongers gather up their victims by dozens and drive them, chained, to the general depot at Baltimore. When a sufficient number have been collected here, a ship is chartered for the purpose of conveying the forlorn crew to Mobile or to New Orleans. From the slave-prison to the ship, they are usually driven in the darkness of night, for since the anti-slavery agitation a certain caution is observed.

In the deep, still darkness of midnight, I have been often aroused by the dead, heavy footsteps and the piteous cries of the chained gangs that passed our door. The anguish of my boyish heart was intense; and I was often consoled, when speaking to my mistress in the morning, to hear her say that the custom was very wicked—that she hated to hear the rattle of the chains, and the heart-rending cries. I was glad to find one who sympathized with me in my horror.

Fellow citizens, this murderous traffic is today in active operation in this boasted republic. In the solitude of my spirit, I see clouds of dust raised on the highways of the South; I see the bleeding footsteps; I hear the doleful wail of fettered humanity, on the way to the slave markets, where the victims are to be sold like horses, sheep, and swine, knocked off to the highest bidder. There I see the tenderest ties ruthlessly broken, to gratify the lust, caprice, and rapacity of the buyers and sellers of men. My soul sickens at the sight.

Is this the land your fathers loved?
The freedom which they toiled to win?
Is this the earth whereon they moved?
Are these the graves they slumber in?

But a still more inhuman, disgraceful, and scandalous state of things remains to be presented. By an act of the American Congress, not yet two years old, slavery has been nationalized in its most horrible and revolting form. By that act, Mason and Dixon's line has been obliterated; New York has become as Virginia; and the power to hold, hunt, and sell men, women, and children as slaves remains no longer a mere state institution, but is now an institution of the whole United States. The power is coextensive with the Star Spangled Banner and American Christianity. Where these go may also go the merciless slave-hunter. Where these are man is not sacred. He is a bird for the sportsman's gun. By that most foul and fiendish of all human decrees, the liberty and person of every man are put in peril. Your broad republican domain is a hunting-ground for men. Not for thieves and robbers, enemies of society, merely, but for men guilty of no crime. Your lawmakers have commanded all good citizens to engage in this hellish sport. Your President, your Secretary of State, your lords, nobles, and ecclesiastics, enforce as a duty you owe to your free and glorious country and to your God, that you do this accursed thing. Not fewer than forty Americans have within the past two years been hunted down, and without a moment's warning, hurried away in chains, and consigned to slavery and excruciating torture. Some of these have had wives and children dependent on them for bread; but of this no account was made. The right of the hunter to his prey stands superior to the right of marriage, and to all rights in this republic, the rights of God included! For black men there are neither law, justice, humanity, nor religion. The fugitive slave law makes mercy to them a crime, and bribes the judge who tries them. An American judge gets ten dollars for every victim he consigns to slavery, and five when he fails to do so. The oath of any two villains is sufficient, under this hell-black enactment, to send the most pious and exemplary black man into the remorseless jaws of slavery! His own testimony is nothing. He can bring no witnesses for himself. The minister of American justice is bound by the law to hear but one side, and that side is the side of the oppressor. Let this damning fact be perpetually told. Let it be thundered around the world that, in tyrant-killing, king-hating, people-loving, democratic, Christian America, the seats of justice are filled with judges who hold their office under an open and palpable bribe, and are bound in deciding in the case of a man's liberty to hear only his accusers!

In glaring violation of justice, in shameless disregard of the forms of administering law, in cunning arrangement to entrap the defenseless, and in diabolical intent, this fugitive slave law stands alone in the annals of tyrannical legislation. I doubt if there be another nation on the globe having the brass and the baseness to put such a law on the statute-book. If any man in this assembly thinks differently from me in this matter, and feels able to disprove my statements, I will gladly confront him at any suitable time and place he may select.

Afterward

In 1845 Frederick Douglass published his autobiography, Narrative of the Life of Frederick Douglass, an American Slave, Written by Himself, *and with the proceeds he purchased his own freedom for $710.96.*

Frederick Douglass died on February 20, 1895.

Selected Reading

Blight, David W., Editor. *Narrative of the Life of Frederick Douglass, an American Slave: Written by Himself.* Boston, MA: St. Martin's Press. 2002.

Kendrick, Paul, and Stephen Kendrick. *Douglass and Lincoln: How a Revolutionary Black Leader and a Reluctant Liberator Struggled to End Slavery and Save the Union.* New York, NY: Walker & Co. 2008.

McFeely, William S. *Frederick Douglass.* New York, NY: Norton. 1991.

William Lloyd Garrison
No Compromise With The Evil Of Slavery
February 14, 1854

William Lloyd Garrison, the preeminent abolitionist editor of his time, was born on December 13, 1805 in Newburyport, Massachusetts. By trade a newspaper editor, Garrison joined the abolitionist cause and found work in Baltimore, Maryland on the influential anti-slavery newspaper, "The Genius of Universal Emancipation." He wrote a column called "The Black List" in which he reported on the barbarities of slavery—kidnappings, whippings, murders. He lost his job and was imprisoned for libeling a slave trader. Returning to Boston, Massachusetts, Garrison founded his own anti-slavery newspaper, "The Liberator," calling for "immediate and unconditional emancipation." Co-founding the American Anti-Slavery Society in 1833, Garrison made sure his views on abolition were heard for the next thirty-five years. This speech, his most famous, was delivered in New York City to the American Anti-Slavery Society.

.... I am a believer in that portion of the Declaration of American Independence in which it is set forth, as among self-evident truths, "that all men are created equal; that they are endowed by their Creator with certain inalienable rights; that among these are life, liberty, and the pursuit of happiness." Hence, I am an abolitionist. Hence, I cannot but regard oppression in every form–and most of all, that which turns a man into a thing–with indignation and abhorrence.... They who desire me to be dumb on the subject of slavery, unless I will open my mouth in its defense, ask me to give the lie to my professions, to degrade my manhood, and to stain my soul. I will not be a liar, a poltroon, or a hypocrite, to accommodate any party, to gratify any sect, to escape any odium or peril, to save any interest, to preserve any institution, or to promote any object. Convince me that one man may rightfully make another man his slave, and I will no longer subscribe to the Declaration of Independence. Convince me that liberty is not the inalienable birthright of every human being, of whatever complexion or clime, and I will give that instrument to the consuming fire. I do not know how to espouse freedom and slavery together. I do not know how to worship God and Mammon at the same time. If other men choose to go upon all fours, I choose to stand erect, as God designed every man to stand. If, practically falsifying its heaven-attested principles, this nation denounces me for refusing to imitate its example, then, adhering all the more tenaciously to those principles, I will not cease to rebuke it for its guilty inconsistency. Numerically, the contest may be an unequal one, for the time being; but the author of liberty and the source of justice, the adorable God, is more than multitudinous, and he will defend the right. My crime is that I will not go with the multitude to do evil. My singularity is that when I say that freedom is of God and slavery is of the devil, I mean just what I say. My fanaticism is that I insist on the American people abolishing slavery or ceasing to prate of the rights of man. My hardihood is in measuring them by their own mouths…

[In] what European nation is personal liberty held in such contempt as in our own? Where are there such unbelievers in the natural equality and freedom of mankind? Our slaves outnumber the entire population of the country at the time of our revolutionary struggle. In vain do they clank their chains, and fill the air with their shrieks, and make there supplications for mercy. In vain are their sufferings portrayed, their wrongs rehearsed, their rights defended. As Nero fiddled while Rome was burning, so the slaveholding spirit of this nation rejoices, as one barrier of liberty after another is destroyed, and fresh victims are multiplied for the cotton field and the auction block. For one impeachment of the slave system, a thousand defenses are made. For one rebuke of the man-stealer, a thousand denunciations of the Abolitionists are heard.…

The reasons adduced among us in justification of slaveholding, and therefore against personal liberty, are multitudinous. I will enumerate only a dozen of them:

1. The victims are black.

2. The slaves belong to an inferior race.

3. Many of them have been fairly purchased.

4. Others have been honestly inherited.

5. Their emancipation would impoverish their owners.

6. They are better off as slaves than they would be as freemen.

7. They could not take care of themselves if set free.

8. Their simultaneous liberation would be attended with great danger.

9. Any interference in their behalf will excite the ill-will of the South, and thus seriously affect Northern trade and commerce.

10. The union can be preserved only by letting slavery alone, and that is of paramount importance.

11. Slavery is a lawful and constitutional system, and therefore not a crime.

12. Slavery is sanctioned by the Bible; the Bible is the word of God; therefore, God sanctions slavery, and the Abolitionists are wise above what is written.

Here, then, are twelve reasons which are popularly urged in all parts of the country, as conclusive against the right of a man to himself. If they are valid, in any instance, what becomes of the Declaration of Independence? On what ground can the Revolutionary war, can any struggle for liberty, be justified? Nay, cannot all the despotisms of the earth take shelter under them?...

But they are not valid. They are the logic of Bedlam, the morality of the pirate ship, the diabolism of the pit. They insult the common sense and shock the moral nature of mankind....

The abolitionism which I advocate is as absolute as the law of God, and as unyielding as his throne. It admits of no compromise. Every slave is a stolen man; every slaveholder is a man stealer. By no precedent, no example, no law, no compact, no purchase, no bequest, no inheritance, no combination of circumstances, is slaveholding right or justifiable. While a slave remains in his fetters, the land must have no rest. Whatever sanctions his doom must be pronounced accursed. The law that makes him a chattel is to be trampled underfoot; the compact that is formed at his expense, and cemented with his blood, is null and void; the church that consents to his enslavement is horribly atheistical; the religion that receives to its communion the enslaver is the embodiment of all criminality. Such, at least, is the verdict of my own soul, on the supposition that I am to be the slave; that my wife is to be sold from me for the vilest purposes; that my children are to be torn from my arms, and disposed of to the highest bidder, like sheep in the market. And who am I but a man? What right have I to be free, that another man cannot prove himself to possess by nature? Who or what are my wife and children, that they should not be herded with four-footed beasts, as well as others thus sacredly related?…

Such is man, in every clime—above all compacts, greater than all institutions, sacred against every outrage, priceless, immortal!

By this sure test, every institution, every party, every form of government, every kind of religion, is to be tried. God never made a human being either for destruction or degradation. It is plain, therefore, that whatever cannot flourish except at the sacrifice of that being, ought not to exist. Show me the party that can obtain supremacy only by trampling upon human individuality and personal sovereignty, and you will thereby pronounce sentence of death upon it. Show me the government which can be maintained only by destroying the rights of a portion of the people, and you will indicate the duty of openly revolting against it. Show me the religion which sanctions the ownership of one man by another, and you will demonstrate it to be purely infernal in its origin and spirit.

No man is to be injured in his person, mind, or estate. He cannot be, with benefit to any other man, or to any state of society Whoever would sacrifice him for any purpose is both morally and politically insane. Every man is equivalent to every other man. Destroy the equivalent, and what is left?...

If the slaves are not men—if they do not possess human instincts, passions, faculties, and powers, if they are below accountability, and devoid of reason; if for them there is no hope of immortality, no God, no heaven, no hell; if, in short, they are what the slave code declares them to be, rightly "deemed, sold, taken, reputed and adjudged in law to be chattels personal in the hands of their owners and possessors, and their executors, administrators and assigns, to all intents, constructions, and purposes whatsoever"—then, undeniably, I am mad, and can no longer discriminate between a man and a beast. But, in that case, away with the horrible incongruity of giving them oral instruction, of teaching them the catechism, of recognizing them as suitably qualified to be members of Christian churches, of extending to them the ordinance of baptism, and admitting them to the communion table, and enumerating many of them as belonging to the household of faith! Let them be no more included in our religious sympathies or denominational statistics than are the dogs in our streets, the swine in our pens, or the utensils in our dwellings. It is right to own, to buy, to sell, to inherit, to breed, and to control them, in the most absolute sense. All constitutions and laws which forbid their possession ought to be so far modified or repealed as to concede the right.

But, if they are men—if they are to run the same career of immortality with ourselves; if the same law of God is over them as over all others; if they have souls to be saved or lost; if Jesus included them among those for whom he laid down his life; if Christ is within many of them "the hope of glory"—then, when I claim for them all that we claim for ourselves, because we are created in the image of God, I am guilty of no extravagance, but am bound, by every principle of honor, by all the claims of human nature, by obedience to Almighty God, to "remember them that are in bonds as bound with them," and to demand their immediate and unconditional emancipation...

36

[None] of the excuses for slaveholding in this country are worthy of the least consideration. The act, in both cases, is essentially the same—equally inhuman, immoral, piratical. Oppression is not a matter of latitude or longitude; here excusable, there to be execrated; here to elevate the oppressor to the highest station, there to hang him by the neck till he is dead; here compatible with Christianity, there to be branded and punished as piracy....

How has the slave system grown to its present enormous dimensions: Through compromise. How is it to be exterminated? Only by an uncompromising spirit. This is to be carried out in all the relations of life—social, political, religious....

Our natural, God-given right of free speech, though constitutionally recognized as sacred in every part of the country, can be exercised in the slaveholding states only at the peril of our lives. Slavery cannot bear one ray of light, or the slightest criticism....

Whatever may be the guilt of the South, the North is still more responsible for the existence, growth and extension of slavery. In her hand has been the destiny of the Republic from the beginning. She could have emancipated every slave, long ere this, had she been upright in heart and free in spirit. She has given respectability, security, and the means of sustenance and attack to her deadliest foe....

With a glow of moral indignation, I protest against the promise and the pledge, by whomsoever made, that if the slave power will seek no more to lengthen its cords and strengthen its stakes, it may go unmolested and unchallenged, and survive as long as it can within its present limits. I would as soon turn pirate on the high seas as to give my consent to any such arrangement.... The issue is clear, explicit, determinate. The parties understand each other, and are drawn in battle array. They can never be reconciled—never walk together—never consent to a truce—never deal in honeyed phrases—never worship at the same altar—never acknowledge the same God. Between them there is an impassable gulf. In manners, in morals, in philosophy, in religion, in ideas of

37

justice, in notions of law, in theories of government, in valuations of men, they are totally dissimilar.

I would to God that we might be, what we have never been—a united people; but God renders this possible only by "proclaiming liberty throughout all the land, unto all the inhabitants thereof." By what miracle can freedom and slavery be made amicably to strike hands?...

In itself, slavery has no resources and no strength. Isolated and alone, it could not stand an hour; and, therefore, further aggression and conquest would be impossible....

These are solemn times. It is not a struggle for national salvation, for the nation, as such, seems doomed beyond recovery. The reason why the South rules, and the North falls prostrate in servile terror, is simply this—with the South, the preservation of slavery is paramount to all other considerations—above party success, denominational unity, pecuniary interest, legal integrity, and constitutional obligation. With the North, the preservation of the Union is placed above all other things—above honor, justice, freedom, integrity of soul, the Decalogue and the Golden Rule—the infinite God himself. All these she is ready to discard for the Union. Her devotion to it is the latest and the most terrible form of idolatry. She has given to the slave power a carte blanche, to be filled as it may dictate, and if, at any time, she grows restive under the yoke, and shrinks back aghast at the new atrocity contemplated, it is only necessary for that power to crack the whip of disunion over her head, as it has done again and again, and she will cower and obey like a plantation slave—for has she not sworn that she will sacrifice everything in heaven and on earth, rather than the Union?

What then is to be done? Friends of the slave, the question is not whether by our efforts we can abolish slavery, speedily or remotely, for duty is ours, the result is with God; but whether we will go with the multitude to do evil, sell our birthright for a mess of pottage, cease to cry aloud and spare not, and remain in Babylon when the command of God is, "Come out of her, my people, that ye be not partakers of her sins, and that ye receive not of her plagues." Let us stand in our lot, "and having done all, to stand." At least, a remnant shall be saved. Living or dying, defeated or victorious, be it ours to exclaim, "No compromise with slavery! Liberty for each, for all, forever! Man above all institutions! The supremacy of God over the whole earth!"

Afterward

When slavery was abolished Garrison ceased publication of "The Liberator" on December 22, 1865 telling his readers, "The object for which "The Liberator" was commenced—the extermination of chattel slavery—having been gloriously consummated, it seems to me specially appropriate to let its existence cover the historic period of the great struggle; leaving what remains to be done to complete the work of emancipation to other instrumentalities (of which I hope to avail myself), under new auspices, with more abundant means, and with millions instead of hundreds for allies. Most happy am I to be no longer in conflict with the mass of my fellow-countrymen on the subject of slavery."

William Lloyd Garrison died on May 24, 1879 and is buried in Boston, Massachusetts.

Selected Reading

Fredrickson, George M. *William Lloyd Garrison.* Englewood Cliffs, NJ: Prentice-Hall. 1968.

Grimke, Archibald H. *William Lloyd Garrison, The Abolitionist.* New York, NY: Negro Universities Press, 1969.

Mayer, Henry. All on Fire: *William Lloyd Garrison and the Abolition of Slavery.* New York, NY: W.W. Norton. 2008.

Merrill, Walter M., and Louis Ruchames, Editors. *The Letters of William Lloyd Garrison.* Cambridge, MA: Harvard University Press. 1981.

Thomas, John L. *The Liberator: William Lloyd Garrison.* Boston, MA: Little, Brown. 1963

Henry David Thoreau
The Fugitive Slave Act
July 4, 1854

Henry David Thoreau, best known for Walden, *his treatise on living a simple, self-sufficient life, was born on July 12, 1817 in Concord, Massachusetts. Educated at Harvard College, Thoreau became the protégé of transcendentalist philosopher Ralph Waldo Emerson, who urged him to keep a journal. Parts of that lifelong journal formed the basis of Thoreau's most important philosophical work,* Civil Disobedience. *The Thoreau household was a safe house for runaway slaves escaping to Canada, with Thoreau himself acting as a "conductor" on the Underground Railroad. In 1854 a runaway slave, Anthony Burns, stowed away on a ship to Boston, having fled captivity in Richmond, Virginia. Pursued by slave catchers, Burns was arrested and imprisoned and, under the Fugitive Slave Act, ordered to be returned to his master. Boston, the hub of the Northern anti-slavery movement, erupted in violent protest, and federal troops were called in and martial law was imposed. Thoreau, who by design lived a very reclusive life, agreed, for one of the few times in his life, to express his opinion publicly. On July 4, 1954 at a meeting of the Massachusetts Anti-Slavery Society in Framingham, Massachusetts, Thoreau delivered this impassioned speech.*

I lately attended a meeting of the citizens of Concord, expecting, as one among many, to speak on the subject of slavery in Massachusetts; but I was surprised and disappointed to find that what had called my townsmen together was the destiny of Nebraska, and not of Massachusetts, and that what I had to say would be entirely out of order. I had thought that the house was on fire, and not the prairie. But though several of the citizens of Massachusetts are now in prison for attempting to rescue a slave from her own clutches, not one of the speakers at that meeting expressed regret for it. Not one even referred to it. It was only the disposition of some wild lands a thousand miles off which appeared to concern them.... There is not one slave in Nebraska; there are perhaps a million slaves in Massachusetts.

They who have been bred in the school of politics fail now and always to face the facts. Their measures are half measures and makeshifts merely. They put off the day of settlement indefinitely, and meanwhile the debt accumulates. Though the Fugitive Slave Law had not been the subject of discussion on that occasion, it was at length faintly resolved by my townsmen, at an adjourned meeting, as I learn, that the Compromise Compact of 1820 having been repudiated by one of the parties, "Therefore ... the Fugitive Slave Law of 1850 must be repealed." But this is not the reason why an iniquitous law should be repealed. The fact which the politician faces is merely that there is less honor among thieves than was supposed, and not the fact that they are thieves.

As I had no opportunity to express my thoughts at that meeting, will you allow me to do so here?

Again it happens that the Boston Courthouse is full of armed men, holding prisoner and trying a Man, to find out if he is not really a Slave. Does any one think that justice or God awaits [the judge's] decision?... Such an arbiter's very existence is an impertinence. We do not ask him to make up his mind, but to make up his pack.

I listen to hear the voice of a Governor, Commander-in-Chief of the forces of Massachusetts. I hear only the creaking of crickets and the hum of insects which now fill the summer air. The Governor's exploit is to review the troops on muster days. I have seen him on horseback, with his hat off, listening to a chaplain's prayer. It chances that that is all I have ever seen of a Governor. I think that I could manage to get along without one. If he is not of the least use to prevent my being kidnapped, pray of what important use is he likely to be to me? When freedom is most endangered, he dwells in the deepest obscurity. A distinguished clergyman told me that he chose the profession of a clergyman because it afforded the most leisure for literary pursuits. I would recommend to him the profession of a Governor.

.... I had thought that the Governor was, in some sense, the executive officer of the state; that it was his business, as a Governor, to see that the laws of the state were executed; while, as a man, he took care that he did not, by so doing, break the laws of humanity; but when there is any special important use for him, he is useless, or worse than useless, and permits the laws of the state to go unexecuted. Perhaps I do not know what are the duties of a Governor; but if to be a Governor requires to subject one's self to so much ignominy without remedy, if it is to put a restraint upon my manhood, I shall take care never to be Governor of Massachusetts. I have not read far in the statutes of this Commonwealth. It is not profitable reading. They do not always say what is true; and they do not always mean what they say. What I am concerned to know is, that that man's influence and authority were on the side of the slaveholder, and not of the slave—of the guilty, and not of the innocent—of injustice, and not of justice.... The worst I shall say of [the Governor] is, that he proved no better than the majority of his constituents would be likely to prove. In my opinion, be was not equal to the occasion.

The whole military force of the state is at the service of a Mr. Suttle, a slaveholder from Virginia, to enable him to catch a man whom he calls his property; but not a soldier is offered to save a citizen of Massachusetts from being kidnapped! Is this what all these soldiers, all this *training*, have been for these seventy-nine years past? Have they been trained merely to rob Mexico and carry back fugitive slaves to their masters?

These very nights I heard the sound of a drum in our streets. There were men *training* still; and for what? I could with an effort pardon the cockerels of Concord for crowing still, for they, perchance, had not been beaten that morning; but I could not excuse this rub-a-dub of the "trainers." The slave was carried back by exactly such as these; i.e., by the soldier, of whom the best you can say in this connection is that he is a fool made conspicuous by a painted coat.

Three years ago, also, just a week after the authorities of Boston assembled to carry back a perfectly innocent man, and one whom they knew to be innocent, into slavery, the inhabitants of Concord caused the bells to be rung and the cannons to be fired, to

42

celebrate their liberty, and the courage and love of liberty of their ancestors who fought at the bridge. As if *those* three millions had fought for the right to be free themselves, but to hold in slavery three million others. Nowadays, men wear a fool's-cap, and call it a liberty-cap. I do not know but there are some who, if they were tied to a whipping-post, and could but get one hand free, would use it to ring the bells and fire the cannons to celebrate *their* liberty. So some of my townsmen took the liberty to ring and fire. That was the extent of their freedom; and when the sound of the bells died away, their liberty died away also; when the powder was all expended, their liberty went off with the smoke.

The joke could be no broader if the inmates of the prisons were to subscribe for all the powder to be used in such salutes, and hire the jailers to do the firing and ringing for them, while they enjoyed it through the grating.

This is what I thought about my neighbors.

Every humane and intelligent inhabitant of Concord, when he or she heard those bells and those cannons, thought not with pride of the events of the 19th of April, 1775, but with shame of the events of the 12th of April, 1851. But now we have half buried that old shame under a new one.

.... Every moment that [Massachusetts] hesitated to set this man free, every moment that she now hesitates to atone for her crime, she is convicted. The Commissioner on her case is God; not Edward G. God, but simply God.

I wish my countrymen to consider that, whatever the human law may be, neither an individual nor a nation can ever commit the least act of injustice against the obscurest individual without having to pay the penalty for it. A government which deliberately enacts injustice, and persists in it, will at length even become the laughing-stock of the world.

Much has been said about American slavery, but I think that we do not even yet realize what slavery is. If I were seriously to propose to Congress to make mankind into sausages, I have no doubt that most of the members would smile at my proposition, and if any believed me to be in earnest, they would think that I proposed something much worse than Congress had ever done. But if any of them will tell me that to make a man into a sausage would be much worse—would be any worse—than to make him into a slave—than it was to enact the Fugitive Slave Law—I will accuse him of foolishness, of intellectual incapacity, of making a distinction without a difference. The one is just as sensible a proposition as the other.

I hear a good deal said about trampling this law under foot. Why, one need not go out of his way to do that. This law rises not to the level of the head or the reason; its natural habitat is in the dirt. It was born and bred, and has its life, only in the dust and mire, on a level with the feet....

Recent events will be valuable as a criticism on the administration of justice in our midst, or, rather, as showing what are the true resources of justice in any community. It has come to this, that the friends of liberty, the friends of the slave, have shuddered when they have understood that his fate was left to the legal tribunals of the country to be decided. Free men have no faith that justice will be awarded in such a case. The judge may decide this way or that; it is a kind of accident, at best. It is evident that he is not a competent authority in so important a case. It is no time, then, to be judging according to his precedents, but to establish a precedent for the future. I would much rather trust to the sentiment of the people. In their vote you would get something of some value, at least, however small; but in the other case, only the trammeled judgment of an individual, of no significance, be it which way it might.

It is to some extent fatal to the courts, when the people are compelled to go behind them. I do not wish to believe that the courts were made for fair weather, and for very civil cases merely; but think of leaving it to any court in the land to decide whether more than three millions of people, in this case a sixth part of a nation, have a right to be freemen or not! But it has been left to the courts of *justice*, so called—to the Supreme Court of the

44

land—and, as you all know, recognizing no authority but the Constitution, it has decided that the three millions are and shall continue to be slaves. Such judges as these are merely the inspectors of a pick-lock and murderer's tools, to tell him whether they are in working order or not, and there they think that their responsibility ends....

The law will never make men free; it is men who have got to make the law free. They are the lovers of law and order who observe the law when the government breaks it.

Among human beings, the judge whose words seal the fate of a man furthest into eternity is not he who merely pronounces the verdict of the law, but he, whoever he may be, who, from a love of truth, and unprejudiced by any custom or enactment of men, utters a true opinion or *sentence* concerning him. He it is that *sentences* him. Whoever can discern truth has received his commission from a higher source than the chiefest justice in the world who can discern only law. He finds himself constituted judge of the judge. Strange that it should be necessary to state such simple truths!

I am more and more convinced that, with reference to any public question, it is more important to know what the country thinks of it than what the city thinks. The city does not *think* much. On any moral question, I would rather have the opinion of Boxboro than of Boston and New York put together.... When, in some obscure country town, the farmers come together to a special town-meeting, to express their opinion on some subject which is vexing the land, that, I think, is the true Congress, and the most respectable one that is ever assembled in the United States.

It is evident that there are, in this Commonwealth at least, two parties, becoming more and more distinct—the party of the city, and the party of the country.... Let us not send to the city for aught more essential than our broadcloths and groceries; or, if we read the opinions of the city, let us entertain opinions of our own.

Among measures to be adopted, I would suggest to make as earnest and vigorous an assault on the press as has already been made, and with effect, on the church. The church has much improved within a few years; but the press is, almost without exception, corrupt. I believe that in this country the press exerts a greater and a more pernicious influence than the church did in its worst period. We are not a religious people, but we are a nation of politicians. We do not care for the Bible, but we do care for the newspaper. At any meeting of politicians—like that at Concord the other evening, for instance—how impertinent it would be to quote from the Bible! how pertinent to quote from a newspaper or from the Constitution! The newspaper is a Bible which we read every morning and every afternoon, standing and sitting, riding and walking. It is a Bible which every man carries in his pocket, which lies on every table and counter, and which the mail, and thousands of missionaries, are continually dispersing. It is, in short, the only book which America has printed and which America reads. So wide is its influence. The editor is a preacher whom you voluntarily support. Your tax is commonly one cent daily, and it costs nothing for pew hire. But how many of these preachers preach the truth? I repeat the testimony of many an intelligent foreigner, as well as my own convictions, when I say, that probably no country was ever ruled by so mean a class of tyrants as, with a few noble exceptions, are the editors of the periodical press in *this* country. And as they live and rule only by their servility, and appealing to the worse, and not the better, nature of man, the people who read them are in the condition of the dog that returns to his vomit.

.... The free men of New England have only to refrain from purchasing and reading these sheets, have only to withhold their cents, to kill a score of them at once....

Are they Americans? are they New Englanders? are they inhabitants of Lexington and Concord and Framingham, who read and support the Boston *Post*, *Mail*, *Journal*, *Advertiser*, *Courier*, and *Times*? Are these the Flags of our Union? I am not a newspaper reader, and may omit to name the worst.

Could slavery suggest a more complete servility than some of these journals exhibit? Is there any dust which their conduct does not lick, and make fouler still with its slime? I do not know whether the *Boston Herald* is still in existence, but I remember to have seen it about the streets when Sims was carried off. Did it not act its part, well-serve its master faithfully! How could it have gone lower on its belly? How can a man stoop lower than he is low? do more than put his extremities in the place of the head he has? than make his head his lower extremity? When I have taken up this paper with my cuffs turned up, I have heard the gurgling of the sewer through every column. I have felt that I was handling a paper picked out of the public gutters, a leaf from the gospel of the gambling-house, the groggery, and the brothel, harmonizing with the gospel of the Merchants' Exchange.

The majority of the men of the North, and of the South and East and West, are not men of principle. If they vote, they do not send men to Congress on errands of humanity; but while their brothers and sisters are being scourged and hung for loving liberty, while—I might here insert all that slavery implies and is—it is the mismanagement of wood and iron and stone and gold which concerns them. Do what you will, O Government, with my wife and children, my mother and brother, my father and sister, I will obey your commands to the letter. It will indeed grieve me if you hurt them, if you deliver them to overseers to be hunted by bounds or to be whipped to death; but, nevertheless, I will peaceably pursue my chosen calling on this fair earth, until perchance, one day, when I have put on mourning for them dead, I shall have persuaded you to relent. Such is the attitude, such are the words of Massachusetts.

Rather than do thus, I need not say what match I would touch, what system endeavor to blow up; but as I love my life, I would side with the light, and let the dark earth roll from under me, calling my mother and my brother to follow.

I would remind my countrymen that they are to be men first, and Americans only at a late and convenient hour. No matter how valuable law may be to protect your property, even to keep soul and body together, if it do not keep you and humanity together.

I am sorry to say that I doubt if there is a judge in Massachusetts who is prepared to resign his office, and get his living innocently, whenever it is required of him to pass sentence under a law which is merely contrary to the law of God. I am compelled to see that they put themselves, or rather are by character, in this respect, exactly on a level with the marine who discharges his musket in any direction he is ordered to. They are just as much tools, and as little men. Certainly, they are not the more to be respected, because their master enslaves their understandings and consciences, instead of their bodies.

The judges and lawyers ... and all men of expediency, try this case by a very low and incompetent standard. They consider not whether the Fugitive Slave Law is right, but whether it is what they call *constitutional*. Is virtue constitutional, or vice? Is equity constitutional, or iniquity? In important moral and vital questions, like this, it is just as impertinent to ask whether a law is constitutional or not, as to ask whether it is profitable or not. They persist in being the servants of the worst of men, and not the servants of humanity. The question is not whether you or your grandfather, seventy years ago, did not enter into an agreement to serve the Devil, and that service is not accordingly now due; but whether you will not now, for once and at last, serve God (in spite of your own past recreancy, or that of your ancestor) by obeying that eternal and only just Constitution, which He, and not any Jefferson or Adams, has written in your being.

The amount of it is, if the majority vote the Devil to be God, the minority will live and behave accordingly—and obey the successful candidate, trusting that, some time or other, by some Speaker's casting-vote, perhaps, they may reinstate God. This is the highest principle I can get out or invent for my neighbors. These men act as if they believed that they could safely slide down a hill a little way—or a good way—and would surely come to a place, by and by, where they could begin to slide up again. This is expediency, or choosing that course which offers the slightest obstacles to the feet, that is, a downhill one. But there is no such thing as accomplishing a righteous reform by the use of "expediency." There is no such thing as sliding up hill. In morals the only sliders are backsliders.

Thus we steadily worship Mammon, both school and state and church, and on the seventh day curse God with [an uproar] from one end of the Union to the other.

Will mankind never learn that policy is not morality, that it never secures any moral right, but considers merely what is expedient? chooses the available candidate—who is invariably the Devil— and what right have his constituents to be surprised, because the Devil does not behave like an angel of light? What is wanted is men, not of policy, but of probity, who recognize a higher law than the Constitution, or the decision of the majority. The fate of the country does not depend on how you vote at the polls—the worst man is as strong as the best at that game; it does not depend on what kind of paper you drop into the ballot-box once a year, but on what kind of man you drop from your chamber into the street every morning.

What should concern Massachusetts is not the Nebraska Bill, nor the Fugitive Slave Bill, but her own slaveholding and servility. Let the state dissolve her union with the slaveholder. She may wriggle and hesitate, and ask leave to read the Constitution once more; but she can find no respectable law or precedent which sanctions the continuance of such a union for an instant.

Let each inhabitant of the state dissolve his union with her, as long as she delays to do her duty.

The events of the past month teach me to distrust Fame. I see that she does not finely discriminate, but coarsely hurrahs. She considers not the simple heroism of an action, but only as it is connected with its apparent consequences. She praises till she is hoarse the easy exploit of the Boston tea party, but will be comparatively silent about the braver and more disinterestedly heroic attack on the Boston Court-House, simply because it was unsuccessful!

Covered with disgrace, the state has sat down coolly to try for their lives and liberties the men who attempted to do its duty for it. And this is called *justice*! They who have shown that they can behave particularly well may perchance be put under bonds for their good behavior. They whom truth requires at present to plead guilty are, of all the inhabitants of the state, preeminently innocent. While the Governor, and the Mayor, and countless officers of the Commonwealth are at large, the champions of liberty are imprisoned.

Only they are guiltless who commit the crime of contempt of such a court. It behooves every man to see that his influence is on the side of justice, and let the courts make their own characters. My sympathies in this case are wholly with the accused, and wholly against their accusers and judges. Justice is sweet and musical; but injustice is harsh and discordant. The judge still sits grinding at his organ, but it yields no music, and we hear only the sound of the handle. He believes that all the music resides in the handle, and the crowd toss him their coppers the same as before.

Do you suppose that that Massachusetts ... is anything but base and servile? that she is the champion of liberty?

Show me a free state, and a court truly of justice, and I will fight for them, if need be; but show me Massachusetts, and I refuse her my allegiance, and express contempt for her courts.

The effect of a good government is to make life more valuable, of a bad one, to make it less valuable. We can afford that railroad and all merely material stock should lose some of its value, for that only compels us to live more simply and economically; but suppose that the value of life itself should be diminished! How can we make a less demand on man and nature, how live more economically in respect to virtue and all noble qualities, than we do? I have lived for the last month—and I think that every man in Massachusetts capable of the sentiment of patriotism must have had a similar experience—with the sense of having suffered a vast and indefinite loss. I did not know at first what ailed me. At last it occurred to me that what I had lost was a country. I had

50

never respected the government near to which I lived, but I had foolishly thought that I might manage to live here, minding my private affairs, and forget it. For my part, my old and worthiest pursuits have lost I cannot say how much of their attraction, and I feel that my investment in life here is worth many per cent less since Massachusetts last deliberately sent back an innocent man, Anthony Burns, to slavery. I dwelt before, perhaps, in the illusion that my life passed somewhere only between heaven and hell, but now I cannot persuade myself that I do not dwell wholly within hell. The site of that political organization called Massachusetts is to me morally covered with volcanic scoriae and cinders, such as Milton describes in the infernal regions. If there is any hell more unprincipled than our rulers, and we, the ruled, I feel curious to see it. Life itself being worth less, all things with it, which minister to it, are worth less. Suppose you have a small library, with pictures to adorn the walls, a garden laid out around, and contemplate scientific and literary pursuits, etc., and discover all at once that your villa, with all its contents, is located in hell, and that the justice of the peace has a cloven foot and a forked tail—do not these things suddenly lose their value in your eyes?

I feel that, to some extent, the state has fatally interfered with my lawful business. It has not only interrupted me in my passage through Court Street on errands of trade, but it has interrupted me and every man on his onward and upward path, on which he had trusted soon to leave Court Street far behind....

I am surprised to see men going about their business as if nothing had happened. I say to myself, "Unfortunates! they have not heard the news." I am surprised that the man whom I just met on horseback should be so earnest to overtake his newly bought cows running away—since all property is insecure, and if they do not run away again, they may be taken away from him when he gets them. Fool! does he not know that his seed-corn is worth less this year, that all beneficent harvests fail as you approach the empire of hell? No prudent man will build a stone house under these circumstances, or engage in any peaceful enterprise which it requires a long time to accomplish. Art is as long as ever, but life

51

is more interrupted and less available for a man's proper pursuits. It is not an era of repose. We have used up all our inherited freedom. If we would save our lives, we must fight for them.

I walk toward one of our ponds; but what signifies the beauty of nature when men are base? We walk to lakes to see our serenity reflected in them; when we are not serene, we go not to them. Who can be serene in a country where both the rulers and the ruled are without principle? The remembrance of my country spoils my walk. My thoughts are murder to the state, and involuntarily go plotting against her.

But it chanced the other day that I scented a white water-lily, and a season I had waited for had arrived. It is the emblem of purity. It bursts up so pure and fair to the eye, and so sweet to the scent, as if to show us what purity and sweetness reside in, and can be extracted from, the slime and muck of earth.... What confirmation of our hopes is in the fragrance of this flower! I shall not so soon despair of the world for it, notwithstanding slavery, and the cowardice and want of principle of Northern men. It suggests what kind of laws have prevailed longest and widest, and still prevail, and that the time may come when man's deeds will smell as sweet.... If Nature can compound this fragrance still annually, I shall believe her still young and full of vigor, her integrity and genius unimpaired, and that there is virtue even in man, too, who is fitted to perceive and love it. It reminds me that Nature has been partner to no Missouri Compromise. I scent no compromise in the fragrance of the water-lily.... In it, the sweet, and pure, and innocent are wholly sundered from the obscene and baleful. I do not scent in this the time-serving irresolution of a Massachusetts Governor, nor of a Boston Mayor. So behave that the odor of your actions may enhance the general sweetness of the atmosphere, that when we behold or scent a flower, we may not be reminded how inconsistent your deeds are with it; for all odor is but one form of advertisement of a moral quality, and if fair actions had not been performed, the lily would not smell sweet. The foul slime stands for the sloth and vice of man, the decay of humanity; the fragrant flower that springs from it, for the purity and courage which are immortal.

Slavery and servility have produced no sweet-scented flower annually, to charm the senses of men, for they have no real life: they are merely a decaying and a death, offensive to all healthy nostrils. We do not complain that they *live*, but that they do not get *buried*. Let the living bury them: even they are good for manure.

Afterward

Thoreau wrote, but did not himself deliver, another famous anti-slavery speech, "A Plea For Captain John Brown," read to a rally in Concord, Massachusetts on October 30, 1859. "This question is still to be settled— this negro question, I mean—the end of that is not yet. I foresee the time when the painter will paint that scene, no longer going to Rome for a subject; the poet will sing it; the historian record it; and, with the Landing of the Pilgrims and the Declaration of Independence, it will be the ornament of some future national gallery, when at least the present form of slavery shall be no more here. We shall then be at liberty to weep for Captain Brown. Then, and not till then, we will take our revenge."

Henry David Thoreau died May 6, 1862 and is buried in Concord, Massachusetts.

Selected Reading

Bloom, Harold, Editor. *Henry David Thoreau.* New York, NY: Chelsea House. 1987.

Hendrick, George, and Willene Hendrick. *Why Not Every Man? African Americans and Civil Disobedience in the Quest for the Dream.* Chicago, IL: Ivan R. Dee. 2005.

Rossi, William J., Editor. *Walden, Civil Disobedience, and Other Writings.* New York, NY: W.W. Norton. 2007.

Charles Sumner
The Crime Against Kansas
May 15, 1856

Charles Sumner, the U.S. Senate's most eloquent enemy of slavery, was born on January 6, 1811 in Boston, Massachusetts. A graduate of Harvard College and Harvard Law School, Sumner, in the 1841 case of Roberts v. The City of Boston, *made before the Massachusetts Supreme Court an impassioned plea for racial equality in public education. In 1848 Sumner was one of the founders of the abolitionist Free Soil Party, whose platform was "No more Slave States and no more Slave Territory" and, in 1851, he won election to the U.S. Senate. On May 30, 1854, over Sumner's strenuous objections, the Kansas-Nebraska Act became law, allowing the residents of the Kansas and Nebraska Territories to vote on whether or not to allow slavery within their borders. The result was "Bleeding Kansas," the name given to the outright war that raged thereafter between pro- and anti-slavery factions over the extension of slavery in those territories. On May 15, 1856 Charles Sumner, outraged by what he termed "The Crime Against Kansas," delivered this speech on the floor of the United States Senate.*

You are now called to redress a great transgression. Seldom in the history of nations has such a question been presented. Tariffs, army bills, navy bills, land bills are important, and justly occupy your care; but these all belong to the course of ordinary legislation. As means and instruments only, they are necessarily subordinate to the conservation of government itself. Grant them or deny them, in greater or less degree, and you will inflict no shock. The machinery of government will continue to move. The state will not cease to exist. Far otherwise is it with the eminent question now before you, involving, as it does, liberty in a broad territory, and also involving the peace of the whole country, with our good name in history for ever more.

Take down your map, sir, and you will find that the territory of Kansas, more than any other region, occupies the middle spot of North America, equally distant from the Atlantic on the east, and the Pacific on the west; from the frozen waters of Hudson's Bay on the north, and the tepid Gulf Stream on the south, constituting the precise territorial center of the whole vast continent. To such advantages of situation, on the very highway between two oceans, are added a soil of unsurpassed richness, and a fascinating, undulating beauty of surface, with a health-giving climate, calculated to nurture a powerful and generous people, worthy to be a central pivot of American institutions. A few short months only have passed since this spacious and mediterranean country was open only to the savage who ran wild in its woods and prairies; and now it has already drawn to its bosom a population of freemen larger than Athens crowded within her historic gates, when her sons, under Miltiades, won liberty for mankind on the field of Marathon; more than Sparta contained when she ruled Greece, and sent forth her devoted children, quickened by a mother's benediction, to return with their shields, or on them; more than Rome gathered on her seven hills, when, under her kings, she commenced that sovereign sway, which afterward embraced the whole earth; more than London held, when, on the fields of Crecy and Agincourt, the English banner was carried victoriously over the chivalrous hosts of France.

Against this territory, thus fortunate in position and population, a crime has been committed, which is without example in the records of the past. Not in plundered provinces or in the cruelties of selfish governors will you find its parallel....

But an audience grander far, of higher dignity, of more various people, and of wider intelligence ... has listened to the accusation, and throbbed with condemnation of the criminal. Sir, speaking in an age of light, and a land of constitutional liberty, where the safeguards of elections are justly placed among the highest triumphs of civilization, I fearlessly assert that the wrongs of much-abused Sicily [scourged by a tyrant Roman governor], were small by the side of the wrongs of Kansas, where the very shrines of popular institutions, more sacred than any heathen altar, have been desecrated; where the ballot-box, more precious than any work, in ivory or marble, from the cunning hand of art has been plundered; and where the cry, "I am an American citizen," has been interposed in vain against outrage of every kind, even upon life itself. Are you against sacrilege? I present it for your execration. Are you against robbery? I hold it up to your scorn. Are you for the protection of American citizens? I show you how their dearest rights have been cloven down, while a tyrannical usurpation has sought to install itself on their very necks!

But the wickedness which I now begin to expose is immeasurably aggravated by the motive which prompted it. Not in any common lust for power did this uncommon tragedy have its origin. It is the rape of a virgin territory, compelling it to the hateful embrace of slavery; and it may be clearly traced to a depraved longing for a new slave state, the hideous offspring of such a crime, in the hope of adding to the power of slavery in the national government. Yes, sir, when the whole world, alike Christian and Turk, is rising up to condemn this wrong, and to make it a hissing to the nations, here in our Republic, force—ay, sir, force—has been openly employed in compelling Kansas to this pollution, and all for the sake of political power. There is the simple fact which you will in vain attempt to deny, but which in itself presents an essential wickedness that makes other public crimes seem like public virtues.

But this enormity, vast beyond comparison, swells to dimensions of wickedness which the imagination toils in vain to grasp, when it is understood that for this purpose are hazarded the horrors of intestine feud not only in this distant territory, but everywhere throughout the country. Already the muster has begun. The strife is no longer local but national. Even now, while I speak, portents hang on all the arches of the horizon threatening to darken the broad land which already yawns with the mutterings of civil war; the fury of the propagandists of slavery, and the calm determination of their opponents, are now diffused from the distant territory over widespread communities, and the whole country, in all its extent—marshaling hostile divisions, and foreshadowing a strife which, unless happily averted by the triumph of freedom, will become war—fratricidal, parricidal war—with an accumulated wickedness beyond the wickedness of any war in human annals, justly provoking the avenging judgment of providence and the avenging pen of history, and constituting a strife, in the language of the ancient writer, more than foreign, more than social, more than *civil*; but something compounded of all these strifes, and in itself more than war....

Such is the crime which you are to judge. But the criminal also must be dragged into day, that you may see and measure the power by which all this wrong is sustained. From no common source could it proceed. In its perpetration was needed a spirit of vaulting ambition which would hesitate at nothing; a hardihood of purpose which was insensible to the judgment of mankind; a madness for slavery which would disregard the Constitution, the laws, and all the great examples of our history; also a consciousness of power such as comes from the habit of power; a combination of energies found only in a hundred arms directed by a hundred eyes; a control of public opinion through venal pens and a prostituted Press; an ability to subsidize crowds in every vocation of life—the politician with his local importance, the lawyer with his subtle tongue, and even the authority of the judge on the bench; and a familiar use of men in places high and low, so that none, from the president to the lowest border postmaster, should decline to be its tool; all these things and more were needed, and they were found in the slave power of our Republic. There, sir, stands the criminal, all unmasked before you.

In now opening this great matter, I am not insensible to the austere demands of the occasion; but the dependence of the crime against Kansas upon the slave power is so peculiar and important, that I trust to be pardoned while I impress it with an illustration which to some may seem trivial. It is related in Northern mythology that the god of Force, visiting an enchanted region, was challenged by his royal entertainer to what seemed a humble feat of strength, merely, sir, to lift a cat from the ground. The god smiled at the challenge, and calmly placing his hand under the belly of the animal with superhuman strength, strove, while the back of the feline monster arched far upward, even beyond reach, and one paw actually forsook the earth, until at last the discomfited divinity desisted; but he was little surprised at his defeat when he learned that this creature, which seemed to be a cat and nothing more, was not merely a cat, but that it belonged to and was a part of the great Terrestrial Serpent, which, in its innumerable folds, encircled the whole globe. Even so the creature whose paws are now fastened upon Kansas, whatever it may seem to be, constitutes in reality a part of the slave power which, in its loathsome folds, is now coiled about the whole land. Thus do I expose the extent of the present contest, where we encounter not merely local resistance, but also the unconquered sustaining arm behind. But out of the vastness of the crime attempted, with all its woe and shame, I derive a well-founded assurance of a commensurate vastness of effort against it and by the aroused masses of the country, determined not only to vindicate right against wrong, but to redeem the Republic from the thralldom of that oligarchy which prompts, directs, and concentrates the distant wrong.

Such is the crime, and such is the criminal, which it is my duty in this debate to expose, and, by the blessing of God, this duty shall be done completely to the end.

The senator from South Carolina [Butler] has read many books of chivalry, and believes himself a chivalrous knight with sentiments of honor and courage. Of course he has chosen a mistress to whom he has made his vows, and who, though ugly to others, is always lovely to him; though polluted in the sight of the world, is chaste in his sight—I mean the harlot, Slavery. For her, his tongue is always profuse in words. Let her be impeached in character, or any proposition made to shut her out from the extension of her wantonness, and no extravagance of manner or hardihood of assertion is then too great for this senator. The frenzy of Don Quixote in behalf of his wench, Dulcinea del Toboso, is all surpassed. The asserted rights of slavery, which shock equality of all kinds, are cloaked by a fantastic claim of equality. If the slave states cannot enjoy what, in mockery of the great fathers of the Republic, he misnames equality under the Constitution—in other words, the full power in the national territories to compel fellow men to unpaid toil, to separate husband and wife, and to sell little children at the auction block—then, sir, the chivalric senator will conduct the state of South Carolina out of the Union! Heroic knight! Exalted senator! A second Moses come for a second exodus!

.... [The] senator, in the unrestrained chivalry of his nature, has undertaken to apply opprobrious words to those who differ from him on this floor. He calls them "sectional and fanatical"; and opposition to the usurpation in Kansas he denounces as "an uncalculating fanaticism." To be sure these charges lack all grace of originality, and all sentiment of truth; but the adventurous senator does not hesitate. He is the uncompromising, unblushing representative on this floor of a flagrant *sectionalism* which now domineers over the Republic, and yet with a ludicrous ignorance of his own position (unable to see himself as others see him) or with an effrontery which even his white head ought not to protect from rebuke, he applies to those here who resist his *sectionalism* the very epithet which designates himself.... I care little for names but, since the question has been raised here, I affirm that the Republican party of the Union is in no just sense *sectional*, but, more than any other party, *national*; and that it now goes forth to dislodge from the high places of the government the tyrannical sectionalism of which the senator from South Carolina is one of the maddest zealots.

.... He shows an incapacity of accuracy whether in stating the Constitution or in stating the law; whether in the details of statistics or the diversions of scholarship. He can not open his mouth but out there flies a blunder....

But it is against the people of Kansas that the sensibilities of the senator are particularly aroused. Coming, as he announces, "from a state"—ay, sir, from South Carolina—he turns with lordly disgust from this newly-formed community, which he will not recognize even as a "body politic." Pray, sir, by what title does he indulge in this egotism? Has he read the history of "the state" which he represents?...

59

[The] senator, to whom that "state" has in part committed the guardianship of its good name, instead of moving with backward treading steps, to cover its nakedness, rushes forward in the very ecstasy of madness, to expose it by provoking a comparison with Kansas. South Carolina is old; Kansas is young. South Carolina counts by centuries, where Kansas counts by years. But a beneficent example may be born in a day; and I venture to say that against the two centuries of the older "state" may be already set the two years of trial, evolving corresponding virtue, in the younger community. In the one is the long wail of slavery; in the other, the hymns of freedom. And if we glance at special achievements, it will be difficult to find anything in the history of South Carolina which presents so much of heroic spirit in an heroic cause as appears in that repulse of the Missouri invaders by the beleaguered town of Lawrence, where even the women gave their effective efforts to freedom.

The matrons of Rome, who poured their jewels into the Treasury for the public defense—the wives of Prussia who, with delicate fingers, clothed their defenders against French invasion—the mothers of our own Revolution, who sent forth their sons, covered with prayers and blessings, to combat for human rights— did nothing of self-sacrifice truer than did these women on this occasion. Were the whole history of South Carolina blotted out of existence from its very beginning down to the day of the last election of the senator to his present seat on this floor, civilization might lose—I do not say how little, but surely less than it has already gained by the example of Kansas in its valiant struggle against oppression, and in the development of a new science of emigration. Already, in Lawrence alone, there are newspapers and schools, including a high school, and throughout this infant territory there is more mature scholarship far, in proportion to its inhabitants, than in all South Carolina. Ah, sir, I tell the senator that Kansas, welcomed as a free state, will be a "ministering angel" to the Republic when South Carolina, in the cloak of darkness which she hugs, "lies howling."

Afterward

On May 22, 1854, outraged by the portions of Charles Sumner's "Crime Against Kansas" speech which had personally attacked South Carolina Senator Andrew Butler, one of the authors of the Kansas-Nebraska Act, South Carolina Congressman Preston Brooks walked into the Senate Chamber and viciously beat Senator Sumner into unconsciousness. Sumner did not return to the Senate for three years and, upon his return, delivered a speech entitled "The Barbarism of Slavery."

Charles Sumner died on March 11, 1874 and is buried in Cambridge, Massachusetts.

Selected Reading

Blue, Frederick J. *Charles Sumner and the Conscience of the North.* Arlington Heights, IL: Harlan Davidson. 1994.

Donald, David H. *Charles Sumner.* New York, NY: Da Capo Press. 1996.

Palmer, Beverly Wilson, Editor. *The Selected Letters of Charles Sumner.* Boston, MA: Northeastern University Press. 1990.

Abraham Lincoln
A House Divided Against Itself
June 16, 1858

On June 16, 1858 the Illinois State Republican Party Convention, meeting in Springfield, unanimously nominated Abraham Lincoln for the United States Senate seat then held by Democrat Stephen A. Douglas. Lincoln, an opponent of the extension of slavery, drew his central theme from Matthew 12:25, "A House Divided Against Itself Cannot Stand," in order to attack Douglas' extension of slavery scheme, known as "Popular Sovereignty."

If we could first know where we are, and whither we are tending, we could better judge what to do, and how to do it.

We are now far into the fifth year since a policy was initiated, with the avowed object and confident promise, of putting an end to slavery agitation. Under the operation of that policy, that agitation has not only not ceased but has constantly augmented. In my opinion, it will not cease until a crisis shall have been reached, and passed—

A house divided against itself cannot stand.

I believe this government cannot endure permanently half slave and half free.

I do not expect the Union to be dissolved—I do not expect the house to fall—but I do expect it will cease to be divided.

It will become all one thing, or all the other.

Either the opponents of slavery will arrest the further spread of it and place it where the public mind shall rest in the belief that it is in course of ultimate extinction; or its advocates will push it forward till it shall become alike lawful in all the states, old as well as new, North as well as South.

Have we no tendency to the latter condition?

Let any one who doubts carefully contemplate that now almost complete legal combination—piece of machinery, so to speak—

compounded of the Nebraska doctrine and the Dred Scott decision. Let him consider not only what work the machinery is adapted to do and how well adapted; but also let him study the history of its construction and trace, if he can, or rather fail, if he can, to trace the evidences of design and concert of action among its chief bosses from the beginning.

The new year 1854 found slavery excluded from more than half the states by state Constitutions and from most of the national territory by Congressional prohibition.

Four days later commenced the struggle which ended in repealing that congressional prohibition. This opened all the national territory to slavery; and was the first point gained.

But, so far, Congress only had acted; and an endorsement by the people, real or apparent, was indispensable to save the point already gained and give chance for more.

This necessity had not been overlooked; but had been provided for, as well as might be, in the notable argument of "squatter sovereignty," otherwise called "sacred right of self-government," which latter phrase, though expressive of the only rightful basis of any government, was so perverted in this attempted use of it as to amount to just this: That if any one man choose to enslave another, no third man shall be allowed to object.

That argument was incorporated into the Nebraska bill itself in the language which follows: "It being the true intent and meaning of this act not to legislate slavery into any territory or state, nor to exclude it therefrom; but to leave the people thereof perfectly free to form and regulate their domestic institutions in their own way, subject only to the Constitution of the United States."

Then opened the roar of loose declamation in favor of "squatter sovereignty," and "sacred right of self-government."

"But," said opposition members, "let us be more specific—let us amend the bill so as to expressly declare that the people of the territory may exclude slavery." "Not we," said the friends of the measure; and down they voted the amendment.

While the Nebraska bill was passing through Congress, a law case involving the question of a Negro's freedom, by reason of his owner having voluntarily taken him first into a free state and then a territory covered by the Congressional prohibition, and held him as a slave for a long time in each, was passing through the U.S. Circuit Court for the District of Missouri; and both Nebraska bill and lawsuit were brought to a decision in the same month of May, 1854. The Negro's name was "Dred Scott," which name now designates the decision finally made in the case.

Before the then next Presidential election, the law case came to and was argued in, the Supreme Court of the United States; but the decision of it was deferred until after the election. Still, before the election, Senator Trumbull, on the floor of the Senate, requests the leading advocate of the Nebraska bill to state his opinion whether the people of a territory can constitutionally exclude slavery from their limits; and the latter answers, "That is a question for the Supreme Court."

The election came. Mr. Buchanan was elected, and the endorsement, such as it was, secured. That was the second point gained. The endorsement, however, fell short of a clear popular majority by nearly four hundred thousand votes, and so perhaps was not overwhelmingly reliable and satisfactory. The outgoing President, in his last annual message, as impressively as possible echoed back upon the people the weight and authority of the endorsement.

The Supreme Court met again; did not announce their decision, but ordered a re-argument.

The Presidential inauguration came, and still no decision of the court; but the incoming President, in his inaugural address, fervently exhorted the people to abide by the forthcoming decision, whatever it might be.

Then, in a few days, came the decision.

The reputed author of the Nebraska bill finds an early occasion to make a speech at this Capitol, endorsing the Dred Scott Decision and vehemently denouncing all opposition to it.

The new President, too, seizes the early occasion of the Silliman letter to endorse and strongly construe that decision, and to express his astonishment that any different view had ever been entertained.

At length a squabble springs up between the President and the author of the Nebraska bill on the mere question of fact, whether the Lecompton Constitution was or was not, in any just sense, made by the people of Kansas; and in that quarrel the latter declares that all he wants is a fair vote for the people, and that he cares not whether slavery be voted down or voted up. I do not understand his declaration that he cares not whether slavery be voted down or voted up, to be intended by him other than as an apt definition of the policy he would impress upon the public mind—the principle for which he declares he has suffered much and is ready to suffer to the end.

And well may he cling to that principle. If he has any parental feeling, well may he cling to it. That principle is the only shred left of his original Nebraska doctrine. Under the Dred Scott decision, "squatter sovereignty" squatted out of existence, tumbled down like temporary scaffolding—like the mold at the foundry served through one blast and fell back into loose sand—helped to carry an election, and then was kicked to the winds. His late joint struggle with the Republicans against the Lecompton Constitution involves nothing of the original Nebraska doctrine. That struggle was made on a point—the right of a people to make their own constitution—upon which he and the Republicans have never differed.

The several points of the Dred Scott decision in connection with Senator Douglas' "care not" policy constitute the piece of machinery in its present state of advancement.

The working points of that machinery are:

First, that no Negro slave, imported as such from Africa, and no descendant of such slave can ever be a citizen of any state, in the sense of that term as used in the Constitution of the United States.

This point is made in order to deprive the Negro, in every possible event, of the benefit of that provision of the United States Constitution, which declares that "the citizens of each state shall be entitled to all privileges and immunities of citizens in the several states."

Secondly, that "subject to the Constitution of the United States," neither Congress nor a territorial legislature can exclude slavery from any United States territory. The point is made in order that individual men may fill up the territories with slaves, without danger of losing them as property, and thus enhance the chances of permanency to the institution through all the future.

Thirdly, that whether the holding a Negro in actual slavery in a free state makes him free, as against the holder, the United States courts will not decide, but will leave to be decided by the courts of any slave state the Negro may be forced into by the master. This point is made, not to be pressed immediately; but, if acquiesced in for a while, and apparently endorsed by the people at an election, then to sustain the logical conclusion that what Dred Scott's master might lawfully do with Dred Scott in the free state of Illinois, every other master may lawfully do with any other one or one thousand slaves, in Illinois or in any other free state.

Auxiliary to all this, and working hand in hand with it, the Nebraska doctrine (or what is left of it) is to educate and mold public opinion, at least Northern public opinion, to not care whether slavery is voted down or voted up.

This shows exactly where we now are, and partially also whither we are tending.

It will throw additional light on the latter, to go back and run the mind over the string of historical facts already stated. Several things will now appear less dark and mysterious than they did when they were transpiring. The people were to be left "perfectly free," "subject only to the Constitution." What the Constitution had to do with it, outsiders could not then see. Plainly enough now, it was an exactly fitted niche for the Dred Scott decision to afterward come in, and declare that perfect freedom of the people to be just no freedom at all.

Why was the amendment, expressly declaring the right of the people to exclude slavery, voted down? Plainly enough now, the adoption of it would have spoiled the niche for the Dred Scott decision. Why was the court decision held up? Why even a Senator's individual opinion withheld, till after the Presidential election? Plainly enough now, the speaking out then would have damaged the "perfectly free" argument upon which the election was to be carried.

Why the outgoing President's felicitation on the endorsement? Why the delay of a reargument? Why the incoming President's advance exhortation in favor of the decision?

These things look like the cautious patting and petting of a spirited horse, preparatory to mounting him, when it is dreaded that he may give the rider a fall.

And why the hasty after endorsements of the decision by the President and others?

We cannot absolutely know that all these exact adaptations are the result of preconcert. But when we see a lot of framed timbers, different portions of which we know have been gotten out at different times and places and by different workmen—Stephen, Franklin, Roger, and James, for instance—and we see these timbers joined together, and see they exactly make the frame of a house or a mill, all the tenons and mortises exactly fitting, and all the lengths and proportions of the different pieces exactly adapted to their respective places, and not a piece too many or too few—not omitting even scaffolding—or, if a single piece be lacking, we see the place in the frame exactly fitted and prepared to yet bring such piece in—in such a case, we find it impossible not to believe that Stephen and Franklin and Roger and James all understood one another from the beginning, and all worked upon a common plan or draft drawn up before the first lick was struck.

It should not be overlooked that, by the Nebraska bill, the people of a state as well as territory were to be left "perfectly free," "subject only to the Constitution." Why mention a state? They were legislating for territories, and not for or about states. Certainly the people of a state are and ought to be subject to the Constitution of the United States; but why is mention of this lugged into this merely territorial law? Why are the people of a territory and the people of a state therein lumped together, and their relation to the Constitution therein treated as being precisely the same?

While the opinion of the Court by Chief Justice Taney in the Dred Scott case and the separate opinions of all the concurring Judges expressly declare that the Constitution of the United States neither permits Congress nor a territorial legislature to exclude slavery from any United States territory, they all omit to declare whether or not the same Constitution permits a state, or the people of a state, to exclude it.

Possibly, this is a mere omission; but who can be quite sure, if McLean or Curtis had sought to get into the opinion a declaration of unlimited power in the people of a state to exclude slavery from their limits, just as Chase and Mace sought to get such declaration, in behalf of the people of a territory, into the Nebraska bill—I ask, who can be quite sure that it would not have been voted down, in the one case, as it had been in the other?

The nearest approach to the point of declaring the power of a state over slavery, is made by Judge Nelson. He approaches it more than once, using the precise idea, and almost the language too, of the Nebraska act. On one occasion his exact language is, "except in cases where the power is restrained by the Constitution of the United States, the law of the state is supreme over the subject of slavery within its jurisdiction."

In what cases the power of the states is so restrained by the U.S. Constitution is left an open question, precisely as the same question as to the restraint on the power of the territories was left open in the Nebraska act. Put that and that together, and we have another nice little niche, which we may, ere long, see filled with another Supreme Court decision, declaring that the Constitution of the United States does not permit a state to exclude slavery from its limits.

And this may especially be expected if the doctrine of "care not whether slavery be voted down or voted up" shall gain upon the public mind sufficiently to give promise that such a decision can be maintained when made.

Such a decision is all that slavery now lacks of being alike lawful in all the states.

Welcome or unwelcome, such decision is probably coming, and will soon be upon us, unless the power of the present political dynasty shall be met and overthrown. We shall lie down pleasantly dreaming that the people of Missouri are on the verge of making their state free; and we shall awake to the reality instead, that the Supreme Court has made Illinois a slave state.

To meet and overthrow the power of that dynasty is the work now before all those who would prevent that consummation. This is what we have to do. But how can we best do it?

There are those who denounce us openly to their own friends, and yet whisper us softly that Senator Douglas is the aptest instrument there is with which to effect that object. They do not tell us, nor has he told us, that he wishes any such object to be effected. They wish us to infer all from the facts that he now has a little quarrel with the present head of the dynasty, and that he has regularly voted with us on a single point, upon which he and we have never differed.

They remind us that he is a great man and that the largest of us are very small ones. Let this be granted. But "a living dog is better that a dead lion." Judge Douglas, if not a dead lion for this work, is at least a caged and toothless one. How can he oppose the advances of slavery? He don't care anything about it. His avowed mission is impressing the "public heart" to care nothing about it.

A leading Douglas Democratic newspaper thinks Douglas's superior talent will be needed to resist the revival of the African slave trade. Does Douglas believe an effort to revive that trade is approaching? He has not said so. Does he really think so? But if it is, how can he resist it? For years he has labored to prove it a sacred right of white men to take Negro slaves into the new territories. Can he possibly show that it is less a sacred right to buy them where they can be bought cheapest? And unquestionably they can be bought cheaper in Africa than in Virginia.

He has done all in his power to reduce the whole question of slavery to one of a mere right of property and, as such, how can he oppose the foreign slave trade—how can he refuse that trade in that "property" shall be "perfectly free"—unless he does it as a protection to the home production? And as the home producers will probably not ask the protection, he will be wholly without a ground of opposition. Senator Douglas holds, we know, that a man may rightfully be wiser today than he was yesterday—that he may rightfully change when he finds himself wrong. But can we, for that reason, run ahead and infer that he will make any particular change, of which he himself has given no intimation? Can we safely base our action upon any such vague inference?

Now, as ever, I wish to not misrepresent Judge Douglas's position, question his motives, or do aught that can be personally offensive to him. Whenever, if ever, he and we can come together on principle so that our great cause may have assistance from his great ability, I hope to have interposed no adventitious obstacle.

But clearly, he is not now with us—he does not pretend to be— he does not promise to ever be. Our cause, then, must be entrusted to and conducted by its own undoubted friends—those whose hands are free, whose hearts are in the work, who do care for the result.

Two years ago the Republicans of the nation mustered over thirteen hundred thousand strong. We did this under the single impulse of resistance to a common danger, with every external circumstance against us. Of strange, discordant, and even hostile elements, we gathered from the four winds, and formed and fought the battle through, under the constant hot fire of a disciplined, proud, and pampered enemy.

Did we brave all then to falter now?—now—when that same enemy is wavering, dissevered, and belligerent? The result is not doubtful. We shall not fail—if we stand firm, we shall not fail.

Wise counsels may accelerate or mistakes delay it, but sooner or later the victory is sure to come!

Afterward

Lincoln became our 16th President. His Presidency spanned the Civil War.

Selected Reading

Harrison, Maureen, and Steve Gilbert, Editors. *Abraham Lincoln: Word for Word.* San Diego, CA: Excellent Books. 1993.

Jaffa, Harry V. *A New Birth of Freedom: Abraham Lincoln and the Coming of the Civil War.* Lanham, MD: Rowman & Littlefield Publishers. 2000.

Johnson, Michael P., Editor. *Abraham Lincoln, Slavery, and the Civil War: Selected Writings and Speeches.* Boston, MA: Bedford/St. Martin's. 2001.

Thomas, John L. *Abraham Lincoln and the American Political Tradition.* 1986.

Stephen Douglas
Popular Sovereignty
August 21, 1858

Stephen Arnold Douglas, know as The Little Giant, *was born in 1813 in Brandon, Vermont. He was admitted to the Illinois bar in 1834, elected to the Illinois State Legislature in 1836, served as Illinois Secretary of State, was appointed to the Illinois Supreme Court, and served in both the U.S. House of Representatives and the U.S. Senate. He proposed the* Kansas-Nebraska Act, *which called for the popular sovereignty that allowed local voters to decide the question of slavery.* Bloody Kansas, *the small-scale civil war that resulted, so tarnished Douglas' reputation that Abraham Lincoln was able to run for his U.S. Senate seat in 1858. On August 21, 1858, in Ottawa, Illinois, Stephen Douglas began the first of seven* Lincoln-Douglas Debates *with this speech on* Popular Sovereignty.

Prior to 1854 this country was divided into two great political parties, known as the Whig and Democratic parties. Both were national and patriotic, advocating principles that were universal in their application. An old-time Whig could proclaim his principles in Louisiana and Massachusetts alike. Whig principles had no boundary sectional line—they were not limited by the Ohio River, nor by the Potomac, nor by the line of the free and slave states, but applied and were proclaimed wherever the Constitution ruled or the American flag waved over the American soil.

So it was, and so it is with the great Democratic party, which, from the days of Jefferson until this period, has proven itself to be the historic party of this nation. While the Whig and Democratic parties differed in regard to a bank, the tariff distribution, the specie circular, and the subtreasury, they agreed on the great slavery question which now agitates the Union. I say that the Whig party and the Democratic party agreed on the slavery question, while they differed on those matters of expediency to which I have referred. The Whig party and the Democratic party jointly adopted the compromise measure of 1850 as the basis of a proper and just solution of the slavery question in all its forms. [Henry] Clay was the great leader, with [Daniel] Webster on his right and [Lewis] Cass on his left, and sustained by the patriots in the Whig and Democratic ranks who had devised and enacted the compromise measures in 1850.

In 1854 Mr. Abraham Lincoln and Mr. Lyman Trumbull entered into an arrangement, one with the other, and each with his respective friend, to dissolve the old Whig party on the one hand, and to dissolve the old Democratic party on the other, and to connect the members of both into an Abolition party, under the name and disguise of a Republican party. The terms of that arrangement between Lincoln and Trumbull have been published by Lincoln's special friend, James H. Matheny, Esq., and they were that Lincoln should have General Shield's place in the United States Senate, which was then about to become vacant, and that Trumbull should have my seat when my term expired. Lincoln went to work to abolitionize the old Whig party all over the state, pretending that he was then as good a Whig as ever; and Trumbull went to work in his part of the state preaching abolitionism in its milder and lighter form, and trying to abolitionize the Democratic party, and bring old Democrats handcuffed and bound hand and foot into the Abolition camp. In pursuance of the arrangement, the parties met at Springfield in October, 1854, and proclaimed their new platform. Lincoln was to bring into the Abolition camp the old-time Whigs, and transfer them over to Giddings, Chase, Fred Douglass, and Parson Lovejoy, who were ready to receive them and christen them in their new faith.

I desire to know whether Mr. Lincoln today stands as he did in 1854, in favor of the unconditional repeal of the Fugitive Slave Law. I desire him to answer whether he stands pledged today, as he did in 1854, against the admission of any more slave states into the Union, even if the people want them. I want to know whether he stands pledged against the admission of a new state into the Union with such a Constitution as the people of that state may see fit to make. I want to know whether he stands today pledged to the abolition of slavery in the District of Columbia. I desire him to answer whether he stands pledged to the prohibition of the slave trade between the different states. I desire to know whether he stands pledged to prohibit slavery in all the territories of the United States, North as well as South of the Missouri Compromise line. I desire him to answer whether he is opposed to the acquisition of any more territory unless slavery is prohibited therein. I want his answer to these questions. Your affirmative cheers in favor of this Abolition platform are not satisfactory.

I ask Abraham Lincoln to answer these questions in order that when I trot him down to lower Egypt, I may put the same questions to him. My principles are the same everywhere. I can proclaim them alike in the North, the South, the East, and the West. My principles will apply wherever the Constitution prevails and the American flag waves. I desire to know whether Mr. Lincoln's principles will bear transplanting from Ottawa to Jonesboro. I put these questions to him today distinctly, and ask an answer. I have a right to an answer, for I quote from the platform of the Republican party, made by himself and others at the time that party was formed, and the bargain made by Lincoln to dissolve and kill the old Whig party, and transfer its members, bound hand and foot, to the Abolition party under the direction of Giddings and Fred Douglass.

In the remarks I have made on this platform, and the position of Mr. Lincoln upon it, I mean nothing personally disrespectful or unkind to that gentleman. I have known him for nearly twenty-five years. There were many points of sympathy between us when we first got acquainted. We were both comparatively boys, and both struggling with poverty in a strange land. I was a schoolteacher in the town of Winchester, and he a flourishing grocery keeper in the town of Salem. He was more successful in his occupation than I was in mine, and hence more fortunate in this world's goods. Lincoln is one of those peculiar men who perform with admirable skill everything which they undertake. I made as good a schoolteacher as I could and, when a cabinet maker, I made a good bedstead and tables, although my old boss said I succeeded better with bureaus and secretaries than with anything else; but I believe that Lincoln always was more successful in business than I, for his business enabled him to get into the Legislature.

I met him there, however, and had sympathy with him, because of the uphill struggle we both had in life. He was then just as good at telling an anecdote as now. He could beat any of the boys wrestling, or running a foot race, in pitching quoits, or tossing a copper—could ruin more liquor than all the boys of the town together, and the dignity and impartiality with which he presided at a horse race or fist fight excited the admiration and won the praise of everybody that was present and participated. I sympathized with him because he was struggling with difficulties, and so was I. Mr. Lincoln served with me in the Legislature in 1836 when we both retired, and he subsided, or became submerged, and was lost sight of as a public man for some years.

In 1846, when Wilmot introduced his celebrated proviso, and the Abolition tornado swept over the country, Lincoln again turned up as a member of Congress from the Sangamon district. I was then in the Senate of the United States, and was glad to welcome my old friend and companion. While in Congress, he distinguished himself by his opposition to the Mexican War, taking the side of the common enemy against his own country; and when he returned home, he found that the indignation of the people followed him everywhere, and he was again submerged or obliged to retire into private life, forgotten by his former friends. He came up again in 1854, just in time to make an Abolition or Black Republican platform, in company with Giddings, Lovejoy, Chase, and Fred Douglass, for the Republican party to stand upon.

These two men, having formed this combination to abolitionize the old Whig party and the old Democratic party, and put themselves into the Senate of the United States, in pursuance of their bargain, are now carrying out that arrangement. Matheny states that Trumbull broke faith—that the bargain was that Lincoln should be the Senator in Shield's place, and Trumbull cheated Lincoln, having control of four or five abolitionized Democrats who were holding over in the Senate; he would not let them vote for Lincoln, which obliged the rest of the Abolitionists to support him in order to secure an Abolition Senator. There are a number of authorities for the truth of this besides Matheny, and I suppose that even Mr. Lincoln will not deny it.

Washington, Jefferson, Franklin, Hamilton, Jay, and the great men of that day made this government divided into free states and slave states, and left each state perfectly free to do as it pleased on the subject of slavery. Why can it not exist on the same principles on which our fathers made it? They knew when they framed the Constitution that in a country as wide and broad as this, with such a variety of climate, production, and interest, the people necessarily required different laws and regulations; what would suit the granite hills of New Hampshire would be unsuited to the rice plantations of South Carolina, and they therefore provided that each state should retain its own Legislature and its own sovereignty, with the full and complete power to do as it pleased within its own limits, in all that was local and not national.

One of the reserved rights of the states was the right to regulate the relations between master and servant on the slavery question. At the time the Constitution was framed, there were thirteen states in the Union, twelve of which were slaveholding states and one a free state. Suppose this doctrine of uniformity preached by Mr. Lincoln—that the states should all be free or all be slave—had prevailed. What would have been the result? Of course, the twelve slaveholding states would have overruled the one free state, and slavery would have fastened by a Constitutional provision on every inch of the American Republic, instead of being left, as our fathers wisely left it, to each state to decide for itself. Here I assert that uniformity in the local laws and institutions of the different states is neither possible nor desirable. If uniformity had been adopted when the government was established, it must inevitably have been the uniformity of slavery everywhere, or else the uniformity of Negro citizenship and Negro equality everywhere.

We are told by Lincoln that he is utterly opposed to the Dred Scott decision, and will not submit to it, for the reason that he says it deprives the Negro of the rights and privileges of citizenship. That is the first and main reason which he assigns for his warfare on the Supreme Court of the United States and its decision. I ask you, are you in favor of conferring upon a Negro the rights and privileges of citizenship? Do you desire to strike out of our state Constitution that clause which keeps savages and free Negroes out of the state, and allow the free Negroes to flow in, and cover your prairies with black settlements? Do you desire to turn this beautiful state into a free Negro colony, in order that when Missouri abolishes slavery she can send one hundred thousand emancipated slaves into Illinois, to become citizens and voters, on an equality with yourselves? If you desire Negro citizenship, if you desire to allow them to come into the state and settle with the white man, if you desire them to vote on an equality with yourselves, and to make them eligible to office, to serve on juries, and to adjudge your rights—then support Mr. Lincoln and the Black Republican party, who are in favor of the citizenship of the Negro. For one, I am opposed to Negro citizenship in any and every form. I believe this government was made on the white basis. I believe it was made by white men for the benefit of white men and their posterity forever; and I am in favor of confining citizenship to white men, men of European birth and descent, instead of conferring it upon Negroes, Indians, and other inferior races.

Mr. Lincoln, following the example and lead of all the little Abolition orators who go around and lecture in the basements of schools and churches, reads from the Declaration of Independence that all men were created equal, and then asks how can you deprive a Negro of that equality which God and the Declaration of Independence award to him? He and they maintain that Negro equality is guaranteed by the laws of God, and that it is asserted in the Declaration of Independence. If they think so, of course they have a right to say so, and so vote. I do not question Mr. Lincoln's conscientious belief that the Negro was made his equal, and hence is his brother; but for my own part, I do not regard the Negro as my equal, and positively deny that he is my brother or any kin to me whatever. Lincoln has evidently learned by heart Parson Lovejoy's catechism. He can repeat it as well as Farnsworth, and he is worthy of a medal from Father Giddings and Fred Douglass for his Abolitionism. He holds that the Negro was born his equal and yours, and that he was endowed with equality by the Almighty, and that no human law can deprive him of these rights which were guaranteed to him by the Supreme Ruler of the universe.

Now, I do not believe that the Almighty ever intended the Negro to be the equal of the white man. If He did, He has been a long time demonstrating the fact. For thousands of years, the Negro has been a race upon the earth, and during all that time, in all latitudes and climates, wherever he has wandered or been taken, he has been inferior to the race which he has there met. He belongs to an inferior race, and must always occupy an inferior position. I do not hold that because the Negro is our inferior therefore he ought to be a slave. By no means can such a conclusion be drawn from what I have said. On the contrary, I hold that humanity and Christianity both require that the Negro shall have and enjoy every right, every privilege, and every immunity consistent with the safety of the society in which he lives. On that point, I presume there can be no diversity of opinion. You and I are bound to extend to our inferior and dependent beings every right, every privilege, every faculty and immunity consistent with the public good.

The question then arises, what rights and privileges are consistent with the public good? This is a question which each state and each territory must decide for itself—Illinois has decided it for herself. We have provided that the Negro shall not be a slave, and we have also provided that he shall not be a citizen, but we protect him in his civil rights, in his life, his person and his property, only depriving him of all political rights whatsoever, and refusing to put him on an equality with the white man. That policy of Illinois is satisfactory to the Democratic party and to me, and if it were to the Republicans, there would then be no question upon the subject; but the Republicans say that he ought to be made a citizen, and when he becomes a citizen he becomes your equal, with all your rights and privileges. They assert the Dred Scott decision to be monstrous because it denies that the Negro is or can be a citizen under the Constitution.

Now, I hold that Illinois had a right to abolish and prohibit slavery as she did, and I hold that Kentucky has the same right to continue and protect slavery that Illinois had to abolish it. I hold that New York had as much right to abolish slavery as Virginia has to continue it, and that each and every state of this Union is a sovereign power, with the right to do as it pleases upon the question of slavery, and upon all its domestic institutions. Slavery is not the only question which comes up in this controversy. There is a far more important one to you, and that is—what shall be done with the free Negro? We have settled the slavery question as far as we are concerned; we have prohibited it in Illinois forever, and in doing so I think we have done wisely, and there is no man in the state who would be more strenuous in his opposition to the introduction of slavery than I would; but when we settled it for ourselves, we exhausted all our power over that subject. We have done our whole duty, and can do no more. We must leave each and every other state to decide for itself the same question.

In relation to the policy to be pursued toward the free Negroes, we have said that they shall not vote, while Maine, on the other hand, has said that they shall vote. Maine is a sovereign state, and has the power to regulate the qualifications of voters within her limits. I would never consent to confer the right of voting and of citizenship upon a Negro, but still I am not going to quarrel with Maine for differing from me in opinion. Let Maine take care of her own Negroes, and fix the qualifications of her own voters to suit herself, without interfering with Illinois, and Illinois will not interfere with Maine. So with the state of New York. She allows the Negro to vote provided he owns two hundred and fifty dollars' worth of property, but not otherwise. While I would not make any distinction whatever between a Negro who held property and the one who did not, yet if the sovereign state of New York chooses to make that distinction, it is her business and not mine, and I will not quarrel with her for it. She can do as she pleases on this question if she minds her own business, and we will do the same thing.

Now, my friends, if we will only act conscientiously and rigidly upon this great principle of popular sovereignty, which guarantees to each state and territory the right to do as it pleases on all things, local and domestic, instead of Congress interfering, we will continue at peace one with another. Why should Illinois be at war with Missouri, or Kentucky with Ohio, or Virginia with New York, merely because their institutions differ? They knew that the North and the South, having different climates, productions, and interests, required different institutions. This doctrine of Mr. Lincoln of uniformity among the institutions of the different states, is a new doctrine, never dreamed of by Washington, Madison, or the framers of this government. Mr. Lincoln and the Republican party set themselves up as wiser than these men who made this government, which has flourished for seventy years under the principle of popular sovereignty, recognizing the right of each state to do as it pleased.

Under that principle we have grown from a nation of three or four millions to a nation of about thirty millions of people; we have crossed the Alleghany Mountains and filled up the whole Northwest, turning the prairies into a garden, and building up churches and schools, thus spreading civilization and Christianity where before there was nothing but savage barbarism. Under that principle we have become, from a feeble nation, the most powerful on the face of the earth, and if we only adhere to that principle, we can go forward increasing in territory, in power, in strength, and in glory until the Republic of America shall be the north star that shall guide the friends of freedom throughout the civilized world. And why can we not adhere to the great principle of self-government upon which our institutions were originally based? I believe that this new doctrine preached by Mr. Lincoln and his party will dissolve the Union if it succeeds.

Afterward

Stephen Douglas defeated Abraham Lincoln in the 1858 Illinois Senate race but The Lincoln-Douglas Debates gained a national reputation for Lincoln. Lincoln received the 1860 Republican Party Presidential nomination. Douglas received the 1860 Democratic Party Presidential nomination. Lincoln defeated Douglas.

Stephen Douglas died on July 3, 1861.

Selected Reading

Guelzo, Allen C. *Lincoln and Douglas: The Debates That Defined America.* New York, NY: Simon & Schuster. 2008.

Morris, Roy, Jr. *The Long Pursuit: Abraham Lincoln's Thirty Year Struggle with Stephen Douglas for the Heart and Soul of America.* New York, NY: Collins. 2008.

Zarefsky, David. *Lincoln, Douglas, and Slavery: In the Crucible of Public Debate.* Chicago, IL: University of Chicago Press. 1990.

William Seward
The Irrepressible Conflict
October 25, 1858

William Henry Seward, one of the great anti-slavery speakers, was born on May 16, 1801 in Florida, New York. He attended Schenectady, New York's Union College and began to practice law in 1822. He served as a New York State Senator, as Governor of New York, and, in 1849, as a U.S. Senator. Two speeches delivered on the floor of the Senate made him famous: his Higher Law *speech, during the debate of Henry Clay's Compromise of 1850, and his* Eternal Conflict *speech, during the debate of Stephen Douglas'* Kansas-Nebraska Act. *On October 25, 1858 in Rochester, New York, while campaigning for the 1860 Republican Presidential nomination, Seward delivered his landmark anti-slavery speech,* The Irrepressible Conflict.

... Our country is a theater which exhibits in full operation two radically different political systems—the one resting on the basis of servile or slave labor, the other on the basis of voluntary labor of freemen.

The laborers who are enslaved are all Negroes, or persons more or less purely of African derivation. But this is only accidental. The principle of the system is that labor in every society, by whomsoever performed, is necessarily unintellectual, groveling, and base, and that the laborer, equally for his own good and for the welfare of the state, ought to be enslaved. The white laboring man, whether native or foreigner, is not enslaved only because he cannot as yet be reduced to bondage.

You need not be told now that the slave system is the older of the two and that once it was universal. The emancipation of our own ancestors, Caucasians and Europeans as they were, hardly dates beyond a period of five hundred years. The great melioration of human society which modern times exhibit is mainly due to the incomplete substitution of the system of voluntary labor for the old one of servile labor which has already taken place.

This African slave system is one which, in its origin and its growth, has been altogether foreign from the habits of the races which colonized these states and established civilization here. It was introduced on this new continent as an engine of conquest and for the establishment of monarchical power by the Portuguese and the Spaniards, and was rapidly extended by them all over South America, Central America, Louisiana, and Mexico. Its legitimate fruits are seen in the poverty, imbecility, and anarchy which now pervade all Portuguese and Spanish America.

The free labor system is of German extraction, and it was established in our country by emigrants from Sweden, Holland, Germany, Great Britain, and Ireland. We justly ascribe to its influences the strength, wealth, greatness, intelligence, and freedom which the whole American people now enjoy. One of the chief elements of the value of human life is freedom in the pursuit of happiness. The slave system is not only intolerable, unjust, and inhuman toward the laborer, whom, only because he is a laborer, it loads down with chains and converts into merchandise, but is scarcely less severe upon the freeman, to whom, only because he is a laborer from necessity, it denies facilities for employment and whom it expels from the community because it cannot enslave and convert him into merchandise also. It is necessarily improvident and ruinous because, as a general truth, communities prosper and flourish, or droop and decline in just the degree that they practice or neglect to practice the primary duties of justice and humanity. The free labor system conforms to the divine law of equality which is written in the hearts and consciences of men, and therefore is always and everywhere beneficent.

The slave system is one of constant danger, distrust, suspicion, and watchfulness. It debases those whose toil alone can produce wealth and resources for defense to the lowest degree of which human nature is capable—to guard against mutiny and insurrection—and thus wastes energies which otherwise might be employed in national development and aggrandizement.

Russia yet maintains slavery and is a despotism. Most of the other European states have abolished slavery and adopted the system of free labor. It was the antagonistic political tendencies of the two systems which the first Napoleon was contemplating when he predicted that Europe would ultimately be either all Cossack or all republican. Never did human sagacity utter a more pregnant truth. The two systems are at once perceived to be incongruous. But they are more than incongruous—they are incompatible. They never have permanently existed together in one country and they never can. It would be easy to demonstrate this impossibility from the irreconcilable contrast between their great principles and characteristics. But the experience of mankind has conclusively established it.

Slavery, as I have already intimated, existed in every state in Europe. Free labor has supplanted it everywhere except in Russia and Turkey. State necessities developed in modern times are now obliging even those two nations to encourage and employ free labor; and already, despotic as they are, we find them engaged in abolishing slavery. In the United States slavery came into collision with free labor at the close of the last century, and fell before it in New England, New York, New Jersey, and Pennsylvania, but triumphed over it effectually and excluded it for a period yet undetermined, from Virginia, the Carolinas, and Georgia. Indeed, so incompatible are the two systems that every new state which is organized within our ever-extending domain makes its first political act a choice of the one and the exclusion of the other, even at the cost of civil war if necessary. The slave states, without law, at the last national election successfully forbade, within their own limits, even the casting of votes for a candidate for President of the United States supposed to be favorable to the establishment of the free labor system in new states.

Hitherto the two systems have existed in different states, but side by side within the American Union. This has happened because the Union is a confederation of states. But in another aspect the United States constitute only one nation. Increase of population, which is filling the states out to their very borders, together with a new and extended network of railroads and other avenues, and an internal commerce which daily becomes more intimate, is rapidly bringing the states into a higher and more perfect social unity or consolidation. Thus these antagonistic systems are continually coming into closer contact and collision results.

Shall I tell you what this collision means? They who think that it is accidental, unnecessary, the work of interested or fanatical agitators, and therefore ephemeral, mistake the case altogether. It is an irrepressible conflict between opposing and enduring forces, and it means that the United States must and will, sooner or later, become either entirely a slaveholding nation or entirely a free labor nation. Either the cotton and rice fields of South Carolina and the sugar plantations of Louisiana will ultimately be tilled by free labor, and Charleston and New Orleans become marts for legitimate merchandise alone, or else the rye fields and wheat fields of Massachusetts and New York must again be surrendered by their farmers to slave culture and to the production of slaves, and Boston and New York become once more markets for trade in the bodies and souls of men.

It is the failure to apprehend this great truth that induces so many unsuccessful attempts at final compromise between the slave and free states, and it is the existence of this great fact that renders all such pretended compromises, when made, vain and ephemeral. Startling as this saying may appear to you, fellow citizens, it is by no means an original or even a modern one. Our forefathers knew it to be true, and unanimously acted upon it when they framed the Constitution of the United States. They regarded the existence of the servile system in so many of the states with sorrow and shame, which they openly confessed, and they looked upon the collision between them, which was then just revealing itself, and which we are now accustomed to deplore, with favor and hope. They knew that either the one or the other system must exclusively prevail.

Unlike too many of those who in modern time invoke their authority, they had a choice between the two. They preferred the system of free labor, and they determined to organize the government and so to direct its activity that that system should surely and certainly prevail. For this purpose, and no other, they based the whole structure of government broadly on the principle that all men are created equal, and therefore free—little dreaming that within the short period of one hundred years their descendants would bear to be told by any orator, however popular, that the utterance of that principle was merely a rhetorical rhapsody, or by any judge, however venerated, that it was attended by mental reservations which rendered it hypocritical and false. By the Ordinance of 1787 they dedicated all of the national domain not yet polluted by slavery to free labor immediately, thenceforth, and forever, while by the new Constitution and laws they invited foreign free labor from all lands under the sun, and interdicted the importation of African slave labor, at all times, in all places, and under all circumstances whatsoever. It is true that they necessarily and wisely modified this policy of freedom by leaving it to the several states, affected as they were by differing circumstances, to abolish slavery in their own way and at their own pleasure, instead of confiding that duty to Congress, and that they secured to the slave states, while yet retaining the system of slavery, a three-fifths representation of slaves in the federal government, until they should find themselves able to relinquish it with safety. But the very nature of these modifications fortifies my position—that the fathers knew that the two systems could not endure within the Union, and expected that within a short period slavery would disappear forever. Moreover, in order that these modifications might not altogether defeat their grand design of a republic maintaining universal equality, they provided that two-thirds of the states might amend the Constitution.

The very Constitution of the Democratic party commits it to execute all the designs of the slaveholders, whatever they may be. It is not a party of the whole Union—of all the free states and of all the slave states; nor yet is it a party of the free states in the North and in the Northwest; but it is a sectional and local party, having practically its seat within the slave states and counting its constituency chiefly and almost exclusively there. Of all its representatives in Congress and in the electoral colleges, two-thirds uniformly come from these states. Its great element of strength lies in the vote of the slaveholders, augmented by the representation of three-fifths of the slaves. Deprive the Democratic party of this strength and it would be a helpless and hopeless minority, incapable of continued organization. The Democratic party, being thus local and sectional, acquires new strength from the admission of every new slave state and loses relatively by the admission of every new free state into the Union.

Afterward

William Seward lost the 1860 Republican Presidential nomination to Abraham Lincoln. He served as U.S. Secretary of State in both the Lincoln and Johnson Cabinets. In 1867 he negotiated Seward's Treaty, the purchase of Alaska.

William Seward died on October 10, 1872.

Selected Reading

Bancroft, Frederic. *The Life of William H. Seward.* Gloucester, MA: P. Smith. 1967.

Donald, David Herbert. *"We Are Lincoln Men": Abraham Lincoln and His Friends.* New York, NY: Simon & Schuster. 2003.

Hale, Edward Everett, Jr. *William H. Seward.* Philadelphia, PA: G.W. Jacobs & Co. 1910.

John Brown
On The Gallows
November 2, 1859

John Brown was born on May 9, 1800 in West Torrington, Connecticut. He dedicated his life to radical abolition, the political movement to end slavery by any means necessary. On October 16, 1859, Brown led twenty-one followers in a raid on the U.S. Arsenal at Harper's Ferry, Virginia. He called unsuccessfully on the slaves in the area to join the fight. The U.S. Marines, commanded by Colonel Robert E. Lee, stormed the arsenal and captured Brown. On October 25 Brown was indicted in a Virginia court on charges of treason, conspiracy, and murder. The trial began the next day and, on October 31, 1859, after forty-five minutes of deliberation, the jury found Brown guilty on all counts. On November 2, 1859, John Brown delivered this speech before the death sentence was imposed.

I have, may it please the Court, a few words to say. In the first place, I deny everything but what I have all along admitted of—a design on my part to free the slaves. I intended certainly to have made a clean thing of that matter, as I did last winter, when I went into Missouri and took slaves without the snapping of a gun on either side, moving them through the country and finally leaving them in Canada. I intended to do the same thing again on a larger scale. That was all I intended. I never did intend murder or treason or the destruction of property, or to excite or incite slaves to rebellion, or to make insurrection.

I have another objection, and that is that it is unjust that I should suffer such a penalty. Had I interfered in the manner which I admit, and which I admit has been fairly proved—for I admire the truthfulness and candor of the greater portion of the witnesses who have testified in the case—had I so interfered in behalf of the rich, the powerful, the intelligent, the so-called great, or in behalf of any of their friends, either father, mother, brother, sister, wife, or children, or any of that class, and suffered and sacrificed what I have in this interference, it would have been all right, and every man in this Court would have deemed it an act worthy of reward rather than punishment. This Court acknowledges too as I suppose the validity of the law of God. I see a book kissed, which I suppose to be the Bible (or at least the New Testament), which teaches me that all things whatsoever I would that men should do to me I should do so to them. It teaches me further to remember them that are in bonds as bound with them. I endeavored to act up to that instruction. I say that I am yet too young to understand that God is any respecter of persons. I believe that to have interfered as I have done, as I have always freely admitted I have done in behalf of his despised poor, I did no wrong, but right. Now, if it is deemed necessary that I should forfeit my life for the furtherance of the ends of justice, and mingle my blood further with the blood of my children and with the blood of millions in this slave country whose rights are disregarded by wicked, cruel, and unjust enactments, I say, let it be done.

Let me say one word further. I feel entirely satisfied with the treatment I have received on my trial. Considering all the circumstances, it has been more generous than I expected. But I feel no consciousness of guilt. I have stated from the first what was my intention and what was not. I never had any design against the liberty of any person, nor any disposition to commit treason or incite slaves to rebel or make any general insurrection. I never encouraged any man to do so, but always discouraged any idea of that kind. Let me say also in regard to the statements made by some of those who were connected with me, I fear it has been stated by some of them that I have induced them to join me. But the contrary is true. I do not say this to injure them, but as regretting their weakness. No one but joined me of his own accord, and the greater part at their own expense. A number of them I never saw, and never had a word of conversation with till the day they came to me, and that was for the purpose I have stated. Now I have done.

Afterward

John Brown was executed on December 2, 1859. Abraham Lincoln, speaking on that day said, We cannot object, even though he agreed with us in thinking slavery was wrong. That cannot excuse violence, bloodshed, and treason. *The war to end slavery, which John Brown wanted and Abraham Lincoln was to lead, began three years later.*

Selected Reading

Abels, Jules, *Man on Fire: John Brown and the Cause of Liberty.* New York, NY: Macmillan. 1971.

Boyer, Richard O. *The Legend of John Brown: A Biography and a History.* New York, NY: Knopf. 1973.

Reynolds, David S. *John Brown, Abolitionist: The Man Who Killed Slavery, Sparked the Civil War, and Seeded Civil Rights.* New York, NY: Alfred A. Knopf. 2005.

Andrew Johnson
Not a Southern Or Any Other Confederacy
December 18, 1860

Andrew Johnson, a pro-Union Southerner, was born on December 29, 1808 in Raleigh, North Carolina. Johnson, by trade a tailor, moved to Greenville, Tennessee, where he became involved in politics, serving as Alderman, Mayor, State Representative, U.S. Congressman, Governor, and Tennessee's U.S. Senator. In the Senate Andrew Johnson was both pro-slavery and pro-Union. Johnson was forced to choose which right was more important to him when, as a result of the election of Abraham Lincoln, South Carolina threatened to secede from the Union. While South Carolina and other slave states agitated for immediate secession and the founding of a Southern Confederacy, Andrew Johnson worked in vain for compromise. On December 8, 1860, while delegates to South Carolina's Secession Convention gathered in Charleston to vote their state out of the Union, Tennessee's Andrew Johnson, the one and only Southern Senator to do so, took to the floor of the United States Senate to deliver this speech, denouncing secession as "treason." The New York Times *headlined this as "Senator Johnson's Great Speech," while* The Chicago Tribune *wrote that Johnson had the honor of "striking the first stunning blow at the treason of the seceding States."*

We are told that certain states will go out and tear this accursed Constitution into fragments, and drag the pillars of this mighty edifice down upon us and involve us all in one common ruin. Will the border states submit to such a threat? No. If they do not come into the movement, the pillars of this stupendous fabric of human freedom and greatness and goodness are to be pulled down, and all will be involved in one common ruin. Such is the threatening language used. "You shall come into our confederacy, or we will coerce you to the emancipation of your slaves." That is the language which is held toward us.

We in the South have complained of and condemned the position assumed by the Abolitionists. We have complained that their intention was to hem slavery in, so that, like the scorpion when surrounded by fire, if it did not die from the intense heat of the scorching flames, it would perish in its own poisonous skin. Now, our sister, without consulting her sisters, without caring for their interest or their consent, says that she will move forward; that she will destroy the Government under which we have lived, and that hereafter, when she forms a government or a constitution, unless the border states come in, she will pass laws prohibiting the importation of slaves into her state from those states, and thereby obstruct the slave trade among the states, and throw the institution back upon the border states, so that they will be compelled to emancipate their slaves upon the principle laid down by the Abolition party. That is the rod held over us!

I tell our sisters in the South that so far as Tennessee is concerned she will not be dragged into a Southern or any other confederacy until she has had time to consider; and then she will go when she believes it to be her interest, and not before. I tell our Northern friends, who are resisting the execution of the laws made in conformity with the Constitution, that we will not be driven on the other hand into their confederacy, and we will not go into it unless it suits us, and they give us such guaranties as we deem right and proper. We say to you of the South we are not to be frightened and coerced. Oh, when one talks about coercing a state, how maddening and insulting to the state; but, when you want to bring the other states to terms, how easy to point out a means by which to coerce them! But ... we do not intend to be coerced.

There are many ideas afloat about this threatened dissolution, and it is time to speak out. The question arises in reference to the protection and preservation of the institution of slavery, whether dissolution is a remedy or will give to it protection. I avow here today that, if I were an Abolitionist, and wanted to accomplish the overthrow and abolition of the institution of slavery in the Southern states, the first step that I would take would be to break the bonds of this Union, and dissolve this Government. I believe the continuance of slavery depends upon the preservation of this Union and a compliance with all the guaranties of the Constitution. I believe an interference with it will break up the Union; and

I believe a dissolution of the Union will, in the end, though it may be some time to come, overthrow the institution of slavery. Hence we find so many in the North who desire the dissolution of these states as the most certain and direct and effectual means of overthrowing the institution of slavery.

What protection would it be to dissolve this Union? What protection would it be to us to convert this nation into two hostile powers, the one warring with the other? Whose property is at stake? Whose interest is endangered? Is it not the property of the border states? Yes; slavery would commence to retreat southward the very moment this Government was converted into hostile powers, and you made the line between the slaveholding and non-slaveholding states the line of division. Then what remedy do we get for the institution of slavery? Must we keep up a standing army? Must we keep up forts bristling with arms along the whole border? This is a question to be considered, one that involves the future; and no step should be taken without mature reflection.

Again, if there is one division of the states, will there not be more than one? I heard a Senator say the other day that he would rather see this Government separated into thirty-three fractional parts than to see it consolidated. I am opposed to the consolidation of Government, and I am as much for the reserved rights of states as any one; but, rather than see this Union divided into thirty-three petty governments, with a little prince in one, a potentate in another, a little aristocracy in a third, a little democracy in a fourth, and a republic somewhere else, a citizen not being able to pass from one state to another without a passport or a commission from his government, with quarreling and warring among the little petty powers, which would result in anarchy—I would rather see this Government today converted into a consolidated government. It would be better for the American people; it would be better for our kind; it would be better for humanity; better for Christianity; better for all that tends to elevate and ennoble man, than breaking up this splendid, this magnificent, this stupendous fabric of human government, the most perfect that the world ever saw, and which has succeeded thus far without a parallel in the history of the world.

I tell our Northern friends that the constitutional guaranties must be carried out, for the time may come when, after we have exhausted all honorable and fair means, if this Government still fails to execute the laws, and protect us in our rights, it will be at an end. Gentlemen of the North need not deceive themselves in that particular; but we intend to act in the Union and under the Constitution, and not out of it. We do not intend that you shall drive us out of this house that was reared by the hands of our fathers. It is our house. We have a right here; and because you come forward and violate the ordinances of this house I do not intend to go out; and if you persist in the violation of the ordinances of the house we intend to eject you from the building and retain the possession ourselves.

Afterward

Soon after this speech, secession was put up for a vote in Tennessee. On June 8, 1861, against the urging of Andrew Johnson who campaigned vigorously against its passage, his home state voted to secede, becoming the eleventh Confederate State. Unlike senators of states that had seceded from the Union, Johnson refused to resign his seat. In 1862, after large parts of Tennessee came back under Union control, President Lincoln named Andrew Johnson Military Governor of Tennessee with the rank of Brigadier General. So successful was he at "reconstructing" Tennessee that Lincoln then chose Johnson as his Vice Presidential running mate in 1864. Disgracing himself at Lincoln's Second Inaugural by delivering, in the words of a spectator, "a drunken foolish speech," Johnson, soon redeemed himself politically in 1865 by delivering a second important speech, Treason Must Be Made Odious, *which can be found on page 147.*

Selected Reading

Bowen, David Warren. *Andrew Johnson and the Negro.* Knoxville, TN: University of Tennessee Press. 1989.

Thomas, Lately. *The First President Johnson: The Three Lives of the Seventeenth President of the United States of America.* New York, NY: Morrow. 1968.

Trefousse, Hans L. *Andrew Johnson: A Biography.* New York, NY: Norton. 1989.

William Tecumseh Sherman
War Is A Terrible Thing!
December 24, 1860

William Tecumseh Sherman was born on February 8, 1820 in Lancaster, Ohio. The Native-American middle name was given him by his father, Judge Robert Sherman, to honor Tecumseh, the great Shawnee War Chief. Throughout his life Sherman was called "Cump" by his friends. His father died when he was nine years old, and in 1836 his foster father, U.S. Senator Thomas Ewing, secured for Sherman an appointment as a cadet at the United States Military Academy at West Point. After graduating in 1840, Sherman served in various military posts. In 1853, after marrying his foster father's daughter and starting a family, Sherman resigned his military commission. He went to work for a bank until its failure in the Panic of 1857. Soon thereafter, through the influence of old military friends, Sherman was offered the position of Superintendent of the newly-formed Louisiana State Seminary of Learning & Military Academy (now Louisiana State University). On December 20, 1860 South Carolina seceded from the Union and secession fever spread throughout the South. On December 24, 1860, with enthusiasm for the imminent secession of Louisiana running high, William Tecumseh Sherman warned his southern friends and colleagues—War Is A Terrible Thing.

You people of the South don't know what you are doing. This country will be drenched in blood, and God only knows how it will end. It is all folly, madness, a crime against civilization! You people speak so lightly of war; you don't know what you're talking about. War is a terrible thing!

You mistake too the people of the North. They are a peaceable people but an earnest people, and they will fight too. They are not going to let this country be destroyed without a mighty effort to save it....

Besides, where are your men and appliances of war to contend against them? The North can make a steam engine, locomotive, or railway car; hardly a yard of cloth or pair of shoes can you make. You are rushing into war with one of the most powerful, ingeniously mechanical, and determined people on Earth—right at your doors.

You are bound to fail. Only in your spirit and determination are you prepared for war. In all else you are totally unprepared, with a bad cause to start with. At first you will make headway, but as your limited resources begin to fail, shut out from the markets of Europe as you will be, your cause will begin to wane. If your people will but stop and think, they must see in the end that you will surely fail.

You people of the South don't know what you are doing. This country will be drenched in blood, and God only knows how it will end. It is all folly, madness, a crime against civilization! You people speak so lightly of war; you don't know what you're talking about. War is a terrible thing!

Afterward

Upon Louisiana's secession, William Tecumseh Sherman resigned from his post as Superintendent of Louisiana State Seminary of Learning & Military Academy. He traveled to Washington, DC to volunteer his services to the U.S. Army. Sherman, rising in rank from Colonel to Major General, practiced what he termed "Hard War," or what is now known as "Total War." To the City Council of Atlanta, Georgia, who were protesting Sherman's "hard war" tactics he bluntly wrote, "You cannot qualify war in harsher terms than I will. War is cruelty, and you cannot refine it; and those who brought war into our country deserve all the curses and maledictions a people can pour out. I know I had no hand in making this war, and I know I will make more sacrifices to-day than any of you to secure peace."

William Tecumseh Sherman died on February 14, 1891 and is buried in St. Louis, Missouri.

Selected Reading

Fellman, Michael, Editor. *Memoirs of General William Tecumseh Sherman*. New York, NY: Penguin Books. 2000.

Kennett, Lee B. *Sherman: A Soldier's Life*. New York, NY: Harper Collins. 2001.

Vetter, Charles E. Sherman: *Merchant of Terror, Advocate of Peace*. Gretna, LA: Pelican Publishing Co. 1992.

Woodworth, Steven E. *Sherman*. New York, NY: Palgrave Macmillan. 2009.

Abraham Lincoln
First Inaugural Address
March 4, 1861

Prior to Abraham Lincoln's Inauguration on March 4, 1861, seven states—South Carolina, Mississippi, Florida, Alabama, Georgia, Louisiana, and Texas—seceded from the Union and formed the Confederate States Of America. In the face of this crisis, Lincoln turned to the works of Andrew Jackson, Daniel Webster, and Henry Clay to form the basis of his Inaugural Address in which he reminded the south: "We are not enemies, but friends."

Fellow-Citizens of the United States: In compliance with a custom as old as the government itself, I appear before you to address you briefly, and to take in your presence the oath prescribed by the Constitution of the United States, to be taken by the President "before he enters on the execution of his office."

I do not consider it necessary at present for me to discuss those matters of administration about which there is no special anxiety or excitement.

Apprehension seems to exist among the people of the Southern states, that by the accession of a Republican Administration, their property, and their peace, and personal security, are to be endangered. There has never been any reasonable cause for such apprehension. Indeed, the most ample evidence to the contrary has all the while existed, and been open to their inspection. It is found in nearly all the published speeches of him who now addresses you. I do but quote from one of those speeches when I declare that "I have no purpose, directly or indirectly, to interfere with the institution of slavery in the states where it exists. I believe I have no lawful right to do so, and I have no inclination to do so." Those who nominated and elected me did so with full knowledge that I had made this, and many similar declarations, and had never recanted them. And more than this, they placed in the platform, for my acceptance, and as a law to themselves, and to me, the clear and emphatic resolution which I now read: "Resolved, That the maintenance inviolate of the rights of the states, and especially the right of each state to order and control its own domestic institutions according to its own judgment exclusively, is essential to that balance of power on which the perfection and endurance of our political fabric depend; and we denounce the lawless invasion by armed force of the soil of any state or territory, no matter under what pretext, as among the gravest of crimes."

I now reiterate these sentiments, and in doing so, I only press upon the public attention the most conclusive evidence of which the case is susceptible, that the property, peace and security of no section are to be in any wise endangered by the now incoming Administration. I add too that all the protection which, consistently with the Constitution and the laws, can be given, will be cheerfully given to all the states when lawfully demanded, for whatever cause, as cheerfully to one section as to another.

There is much controversy about the delivering up of fugitives from service or labor. The clause I now read is as plainly written in the Constitution as any other of its provisions: "No person held to service or labor in one state, under the laws thereof, escaping into another, shall, in consequence of any law or regulation therein, be discharged from such service or labor, but shall be delivered up on claim of the party to whom such service or labor may be due."

It is scarcely questioned that this provision was intended by those who made it, for the reclaiming of what we call fugitive slaves; and the intention of the law-giver is the law. All members of Congress swear their support to the whole Constitution, to this provision as much as to any other. To the proposition, then, that slaves whose cases come within the terms of this clause "shall be delivered up," their oaths are unanimous. Now, if they would make the effort in good temper, could they not, with nearly equal unanimity, frame and pass a law, by means of which to keep good that unanimous oath?

There is some difference of opinion whether this clause should be enforced by national or by state authority; but surely that difference is not a very material one. If the slave is to be surrendered, it can be of but little consequence to him, or to others, by which authority it is done. And should any one, in any case, be content that his oath shall go unkept, on a merely unsubstantial controversy as to how it shall be kept?

Again, in any law upon this subject, ought not all the safeguards of liberty known in civilized and humane jurisprudence to be introduced, so that a free man be not, in any case, surrendered as a slave? And might it not be well, at the same time, to provide by law for the enforcement of that clause in the Constitution which guarantees that "the citizens of each state shall be entitled to all privileges and immunities of citizens in the several states?"

I take the official oath today, with no mental reservations, and with no purpose to construe the Constitution or laws, by any hypercritical rules. And while I do not choose now to specify particular acts of Congress as proper to be enforced, I do suggest that it will be much safer for all, both in official and private stations, to conform to, and abide by, all those acts which stand unrepealed, than to violate any of them, trusting to find impunity in having them held to be unconstitutional.

It is seventy-two years since the first inauguration of a President under our national Constitution. During that period fifteen different and greatly distinguished citizens have, in succession, administered the executive branch of the government. They have conducted it through many perils and, generally, with great success. Yet, with all this scope of precedent, I now enter upon the same task for the brief constitutional term of four years, under great and peculiar difficulty. A disruption of the Federal Union, heretofore only menaced, is now formidably attempted.

I hold that in contemplation of universal law, and of the Constitution, the Union of these states is perpetual. Perpetuity is implied, if not expressed, in the fundamental law of all national governments. It is safe to assert that no government proper ever had a provision in its organic law for its own termination. Continue to execute all the express provisions of our national Constitution, and the Union will endure forever, it being impossible to destroy it except by some action not provided for in the instrument itself.

Again, if the United States be not a government proper, but an association of states in the nature of contract merely, can it, as a contract, be peaceably unmade, by less than all the parties who made it? One party to a contract may violate it—break it, so to speak—but does it not require all to lawfully rescind it?

Descending from these general principles, we find the proposition that, in legal contemplation, the Union is perpetual, confirmed by the history of the Union itself. The Union is much older than the Constitution. It was formed in fact by the Articles of Association in 1774. It was matured and continued by the Declaration of Independence in 1776. It was further matured and the faith of all the then thirteen states expressly plighted and engaged that it should be perpetual by the Articles of Confederation in 1778. And finally, in 1787, one of the declared objects for ordaining and establishing the Constitution was "to form a more perfect Union."

But if the destruction of the Union, by one, or by a part only, of the states be lawfully possible, the Union is *less* perfect than before the Constitution, having lost the vital element of perpetuity.

It follows from these views that no state, upon its own mere motion, can lawfully get out of the Union—that resolves and ordinances to that effect are legally void, and that acts of violence, within any state or states, against the authority of the United States are insurrectionary or revolutionary, according to circumstances.

I therefore consider that in view of the Constitution and the laws, the Union is unbroken; and to the extent of my ability I shall take care, as the Constitution itself expressly enjoins upon me, that the laws of the Union be faithfully executed in all the states. Doing this I deem to be only a simple duty on my part; and I shall perform it, so far as practicable, unless my rightful masters, the

American people, shall withhold the requisite means or, in some authoritative manner, direct the contrary. I trust this will not be regarded as a menace, but only as the declared purpose of the Union that it will constitutionally defend and maintain itself.

In doing this there needs to be no bloodshed or violence; and there shall be none, unless it be forced upon the national authority. The power confided to me will be used to hold, occupy, and possess the property and places belonging to the government, and to collect the duties and imposts; but beyond what may be necessary for these objects, there will be no invasion—no using of force against or among the people anywhere. Where hostility to the United States, in any interior locality, shall be so great and so universal as to prevent competent resident citizens from holding the Federal offices, there will be no attempt to force obnoxious strangers among the people for that object. While the strict legal right may exist in the government to enforce the exercise of these offices, the attempt to do so would be so irritating, and so nearly impracticable with all, that I deem it better to forego, for the time, the uses of such offices.

The mails, unless repelled, will continue to be furnished in all parts of the Union. So far as possible, the people everywhere shall have that sense of perfect security which is most favorable to calm thought and reflection. The course here indicated will be followed, unless current events and experience shall show a modification or change to be proper; and in every case and exigency my best discretion will be exercised according to circumstances actually existing, and with a view and a hope of a peaceful solution of the national troubles, and the restoration of fraternal sympathies and affections.

That there are persons in one section or another who seek to destroy the Union at all events, and are glad of any pretext to do it, I will neither affirm or deny; but if there be such, I need address no word to them. To those, however, who really love the Union, may I not speak?

Before entering upon so grave a matter as the destruction of our national fabric, with all its benefits, its memories and its hopes, would it not be wise to ascertain precisely why we do it? Will you hazard so desperate a step, while there is any possibility that any portion of the ills you fly from have no real existence? Will you, while the certain ills you fly to are greater than all the real ones you fly from? Will you risk the commission of so fearful a mistake?

All profess to be content in the Union, if all constitutional rights can be maintained. Is it true then that any right plainly written in the Constitution has been denied? I think not. Happily the human mind is so constituted that no party can reach to the audacity of doing this. Think, if you can, of a single instance in which a plainly written provision of the Constitution has ever been denied. If, by the mere force of numbers, a majority should deprive a minority of any clearly written constitutional right, it might, in a moral point of view, justify revolution—certainly would, if such a right were a vital one. But such is not our case. All the vital rights of minorities, and of individuals, are so plainly assured to them, by affirmations and negations, guarantees and prohibitions, in the Constitution, that controversies never arise concerning them. But no organic law can ever be framed with a provision specifically applicable to every question which may occur in practical administration. No foresight can anticipate, nor any document of reasonable length contain express provisions for all possible questions. Shall fugitives from labor be surrendered by national or by state authority? The Constitution does not expressly say. May Congress prohibit slavery in the territories? The Constitution does not expressly say. Must Congress protect slavery in the territories? The Constitution does not expressly say.

From questions of this class spring all our constitutional controversies, and we divide upon them into majorities and minorities. If the minority will not acquiesce, the majority must, or the government must cease. There is no other alternative, for continuing the government is acquiescence on one side or the other. If a minority, in such case, will secede rather than acquiesce, they make a precedent which, in turn, will divide and ruin them, for a minority of their own will secede from them whenever a majority refuses to be controlled by such minority. For instance, why may not any portion of a new confederacy, a year or two hence, arbitrarily secede again, precisely as portions of the present Union now claim to secede from it? All who cherish disunion sentiments are now being educated to the exact temper of doing this.

Is there such perfect identity of interests among the states to compose a new Union as to produce harmony only and prevent renewed secession?

Plainly, the central idea of secession is the essence of anarchy. A majority, held in restraint by constitutional checks and limitations, and always changing easily with deliberate changes of popular opinions and sentiments, is the only true sovereign of a free people. Whoever rejects it does, of necessity, fly to anarchy or to despotism. Unanimity is impossible; the rule of a minority, as a permanent arrangement, is wholly inadmissible, so that, rejecting the majority principle, anarchy or despotism in some form is all that is left.

I do not forget the position assumed by some, that constitutional questions are to be decided by the Supreme Court; nor do I deny that such decisions must be binding in any case, upon the parties to a suit, as to the object of that suit, while they are also entitled to very high respect and consideration in all parallel cases by all other departments of the government. And while it is obviously possible that such decision may be erroneous in any given case, still the evil effect following it, being limited to that particular case, with the chance that it may be overruled, and never become a precedent for other cases, can better be borne than could the evils of a different practice. At the same time, the candid citizen must confess that if the policy of the government upon vital questions, affecting the whole people, is to be irrevocably fixed by decisions of the Supreme Court the instant they are made, in ordinary litigation between parties, in personal actions, the people will have ceased to be their own rulers, having to that extent practically resigned their government into the hands of that eminent tribunal. Nor is there in this view any assault upon the court or the judges. It is a duty from which they may not shrink, to decide cases properly brought before them; and it is no fault of theirs if others seek to turn their decisions to political purposes.

One section of our country believes slavery is right, and ought to be extended, while the other believes it is wrong, and ought not to be extended. This is the only substantial dispute. The fugitive slave clause of the Constitution, and the law for the suppression of the foreign slave trade, are each as well enforced, perhaps, as any law can ever be in a community where the moral sense of the people imperfectly supports the law itself. The great body of the people abide by the dry legal obligation in both cases, and a few break over in each. This, I think, cannot be perfectly cured; and it would be worse in both cases *after* the separation of the sections than before. The foreign slave trade, now imperfectly suppressed, would be ultimately revived without restriction, in one section, while fugitive slaves, now only partially surrendered, would not be surrendered at all, by the other.

Physically speaking, we cannot separate. We cannot remove our respective sections from each other, nor build an impassable wall between them. A husband and wife may be divorced, and go out of the presence, and beyond the reach of each other; but the different parts of our country cannot do this. They cannot but remain face to face; and intercourse, either amicable or hostile, must continue between them. Is it possible, then, to make that intercourse more advantageous or more satisfactory *after* separation than *before*? Can aliens make treaties easier than friends can make laws? Can treaties be more faithfully enforced between aliens than laws can among friends? Suppose you go to war, you cannot fight always; and when, after much loss on both sides, and no gain on either, you cease fighting, the identical old questions, as to terms of intercourse, are again upon you.

This country, with its institutions, belongs to the people who inhabit it. Whenever they shall grow weary of the existing government, they can exercise their constitutional right of amending it, or their revolutionary right to dismember or overthrow it. I cannot be ignorant of the fact that many worthy and patriotic citizens are desirous of having the national Constitution amended. While I make no recommendation of amendments, I fully recognize the rightful authority of the people over the whole subject to be exercised in either of the modes prescribed in the instrument itself; and I should under existing circumstances favor rather than oppose a fair opportunity being afforded the people to act upon it.

I will venture to add that to me the Convention mode seems preferable, in that it allows amendments to originate with the people themselves, instead of only permitting them to take or reject propositions, originated by others, not especially chosen for the purpose, and which might not be precisely such as they would wish to either accept or refuse.

I understand a proposed amendment to the Constitution, which amendment, however, I have not seen, has passed Congress, to the effect that the federal government shall never interfere with the domestic institutions of the states, including that of persons held to service. To avoid misconstruction of what I have said, I depart from my purpose not to speak of particular amendments, so far as to say that holding such a provision to now be implied constitutional law, I have no objection to its being made express and irrevocable.

The Chief Magistrate derives all his authority from the people, and they have conferred none upon him to fix terms for the separation of the states. The people themselves can do this also if they choose; but the executive, as such, has nothing to do with it. His duty is to administer the present government, as it came to his hands, and to transmit it, unimpaired by him, to his successor.

Why should there not be a patient confidence in the ultimate justice of the people? Is there any better or equal hope in the world? In our present differences, is either party without faith of being in the right? If the Almighty Ruler of nations, with his eternal truth and justice, be on your side of the North or on yours of the

107

South, that truth, and that justice, will surely prevail, by the judgment of this great tribunal, the American people.

By the frame of the government under which we live, this same people have wisely given their public servants but little power for mischief, and have, with equal wisdom, provided for the return of that little to their own hands at very short intervals. While the people retain their virtue and vigilance, no administration, by any extreme of wickedness or folly, can very seriously injure the government in the short space of four years.

My countrymen, one and all, think calmly and well upon this whole subject. Nothing valuable can be lost by taking time. If there be an object to hurry any of you, in hot haste, to a step which you would never take deliberately, that object will be frustrated by taking time; but no good object can be frustrated by it. Such of you as are now dissatisfied still have the old Constitution unimpaired—and, on the sensitive point, the laws of your own framing under it—while the new administration will have no immediate power, if it would, to change either. If it were admitted that you who are dissatisfied hold the right side in the dispute, there still is no single good reason for precipitate action. Intelligence, patriotism, Christianity, and a firm reliance on Him, who has never yet forsaken this favored land, are still competent to adjust, in the best way, all our present difficulty.

In your hands, my dissatisfied fellow countrymen, and not in mine, is the momentous issue of civil war. The government will not assail you. You can have no conflict, without being yourselves the aggressors. You have no oath registered in Heaven to destroy the government, while I shall have the most solemn one to "preserve, protect, and defend" it.

I am loath to close. We are not enemies, but friends. We must not be enemies. Though passion may have strained, it must not break our bonds of affection. The mystic chords of memory, stretching from every battlefield and patriot grave to every living heart and hearthstone all over this broad land, will yet swell the chorus of the Union, when again touched, as surely they will be, by the better angels of our nature.

Afterward

Lincoln's Presidency spanned the Civil War. He was assassinated by John Wilkes Booth in April 1863.

Selected Reading

Gienapp, William E. *Abraham Lincoln and Civil War America: A Biography.* New York, NY: Oxford University Press. 2002.

Harrison, Maureen, and Steve Gilbert, Editors. *Abraham Lincoln: Word for Word.* San Diego, CA: Excellent Books, 1993.

Lee, Andrew. *Lincoln.* 1989.

Paludan, Phillip S. *The Presidency of Abraham Lincoln.* Lawrence, KS: University of Kansas Press. 1994.

Angelina Grimké Weld
My Country Is Bleeding
May 14, 1863

Angelina Grimké, daughter of a slave owner, was born in Charleston, South Carolina on February 20, 1805. "From her earliest age," her husband would write, "her sympathies were with the cruelly treated race around her, and she was unspeakably shocked by the terrible punishments inflicted on them." Angelina, along with her sister Sarah, fled from Charleston and moved to Philadelphia. In 1833 Grimké joined the American Anti-Slavery Society and in 1836 they published her pamphlet, "An Appeal To The Christian Women Of The South," urging Southern women to work for abolition. In 1838 Grimké married the abolitionist Theodore Weld and they, along with her sister Sarah, edited "American Slavery as it Is: Testimony of a Thousand Witnesses." Grimké Weld's eloquent and passionate speeches on the cruelty of slavery, all based upon her own experience, soon made her a leading speaker for the abolitionist cause. Angelina Grimké Weld's most famous speech on the abolition of slavery was made in New York City to the Women's Loyal National League, in support of a proposed constitutional amendment abolishing slavery forever.

I came here with no desire and no intention to speak; but my heart is full, my country is bleeding, my people are perishing around me. But I feel as a South Carolinian, I am bound to tell the North, go on! go on! Never falter, never abandon the principles which you have adopted. I could but say thus when it was proclaimed in the Northern states that the Union was all that we sought. No, my friends, such a Union as we had then, God be praised that it has perished. Oh, never for one moment consent that such a Union should be reestablished in our land.

There was a time when I looked upon the Fathers of the Revolution with the deepest sorrow and the keenest reproach. I said to their shadows in another world, "Why did you leave this accursed system of slavery for us to suffer and die under? Why did you not, with a stroke of the pen, determine—when you acquired your own independence—that the principles which you adopted in the Declaration of Independence should be a shield of protection to every man, whether he be slave or whether he be free?"

But, my friends, the experience of sixty years has shown me that the fruit grows slowly. I look back and see that great Sower of the world, as he traveled the streets of Jerusalem and dropped the precious seed, "Do unto others as ye would that others should do unto you." I look at all the contests of different nations and see that, whether it were the Patricians of Rome, England, France, or any part of Europe, every battle fought gained something to freedom. Our fathers, driven out by the oppression of England, came to this country and planted that little seed of liberty upon the soil of New England. When our Revolution took place, that seed was only in the process of sprouting. You must recollect that our Declaration of Independence was the very first National evidence of the great doctrine of brotherhood and equality. I verily believe that those who were the true lovers of liberty did all they could at that time. In their debates in the Convention they denounced slavery—they protested against the hypocrisy and inconsistency of a nation declaring such glorious truths, and then trampling them underfoot by enslaving the poor and oppressed, because he had a skin not colored like their own, as though a man's skin should make any difference in the recognition of his rights, any more than the color of his hair or his eyes.

This little blade sprouted as it were from the precious seeds that were planted by Jesus of Nazareth. But, my friends, if it took eighteen hundred years to bring forth the little blade which was seen in our Declaration, are we not unreasonable to suppose that more could have been done than has been done—looking at the imperfection of human nature, looking at the selfishness of man, looking at his desire for wealth and his greed for glory?

Had the South yielded at that time to the freemen of the North, we should have had a free Government; but it was impossible to overcome the long and strong prejudices of the South in favor of slavery. I know what the South is. I lived there the best part of my life. I never could talk against slavery without making my friends angry—never. When they thought the day was far off, and

111

there was no danger of emancipation, they were willing to admit it was an evil; but when God in His providence raised up in this country an Anti-Slavery Society, protesting against the oppressions of the colored man, they began to feel that truth which is more powerful than arms—that truth which is the only banner under which we can successfully fight. They were comparatively quiet till they found, in the election of Mr. Lincoln, the scepter had actually departed from them. His election took place on the ground that slavery was not to be extended, that it must not pass into the territories. This was what alarmed them. They saw that if the National Government should take one such step, it never would stop there, that this principle had never before been acknowledged by those who had any power in the nation.

God be praised. Abolitionists never sought place or power. All they asked was freedom; all they wanted was that the white man should take his foot off the Negro's neck. The South determined to resist the election of Mr. Lincoln. They determined if Fremont was elected, they would rebel. And this rebellion is like their own Republic, as they call it; it is founded upon slavery. As I asked one of my friends one day, "What are you rebelling for? The North never made any laws for you that they have not cheerfully obeyed themselves. What is the trouble between us?" Slavery, slavery is the trouble. Slavery is a "divine institution." My friends, it is a fact that the South has incorporated slavery into her religion; that is the most fearful thing in this rebellion. They are fighting, verily believing that they are doing God service. Most of them have never seen the North. They understand very little of the working of our institutions; but their politicians are stung to the quick by the prosperity of the North. They see that the institution which they have established cannot make them wealthy, cannot make them happy, cannot make them respected in the world at large, and their motto is, "Rule or ruin."

.... I am deeply interested in this colony of Liberia. I do not want it to be cursed with the aristocracy of the South, or any other aristocracy, and far less with the Copperheadism of the North. If these Southern aristocrats are to be colonized, ... don't you think

112

England is the best place for them? England is the country which has sympathized most deeply with them. She has allowed vessels to be built to prey upon our commerce; she has sent them arms and ammunition, and everything she could send through the West India Islands. Shall we send men to Liberia, who are ready to tread the black men under their feet? No. God bless Liberia for what she has done, and what she is destined to do.

…. The men who go there are freemen—citizens; the burdens of society are upon them; and they feel that they must begin to educate themselves, and they are self-educated men. The President of Liberia, Mr. Benson, was a slave about seven years ago on a plantation in this country. He went to Liberia. He was a man of uncommon talents. He educated himself to the duties which he found himself called upon to perform as a citizen. And when Mr. Benson visited England a year ago, he had a perfect ovation. The white ladies and gentlemen of England, those who were really anti-slavery in their feelings—who love liberty—followed him wherever he went. They opened their houses, they had their soirees, and they welcomed him by every kind of demonstration of their good wishes for Liberia.

… [The] great object that I had in view in rising was to give you a representative from South Carolina…. I once had a brother who, … many years ago, during the time of nullification in 1832, was in the Senate of South Carolina, and delivered an able address, in which he discussed these very points, and showed that the South had no right of secession—that, in becoming an integral part of the United States, they had themselves voluntarily surrendered that right. And he remarked, "If you persist in this contest, you will be like a girdled tree, which must perish and die. You cannot stand."

Afterward

Angelina Grimké Weld died on October 26, 1879 in Hyde Park, Massachusetts. The abolitionist leader Wendell Philips summed up her achievements, "I well remember, evening after evening, listening to eloquence such as never then had been heard from a woman. Her own hard experience, the long, lonely, intellectual and moral struggle from which she came out the conqueror, had ripened her power, and her wondrous facility of laying bare her own heart to reach the hearts of others shone forth until she carried us all captive."

Selected Reading

Berkin, Carol. *Civil War Wives: The Lives and Times of Angelina Grimke Weld, Varena Howell Davis, and Julia Dent Grant.* New York, NY: Knopf. 2009.

Browne, Stephen H. *Angelina Grimke: Rhetoric, Identity, and the Radical Imagination.* East Lansing, MI: Michigan State University Press. 1999.

Herron, Carolivia, Editor. *Selected Works of Angelina Grimke Weld.* New York, NY: Oxford University Press. 1991.

Sojourner Truth
The Great Sin of Prejudice Against Color
June 12, 1863

The African American woman who would one day re-christen herself Sojourner Truth was born about 1797 in Ulster County, New York and given the slave name Isabella. Taken from her parents, Isabella was sold to a local slave-holding family in 1810 for the price of $175. Isabella became a runaway slave in 1826—"I did not run off, for I thought that wicked, but I walked off, believing that to be all right"—and finally became a free woman on July 4, 1827, when New York State abolished slavery. In 1843 Isabella experienced a life changing religious conversion—"God gave me the name Sojourner because I was to travel up and down the land showing people their sins and the name Truth because I was to proclaim truth to the people." Sojourner Truth became a traveling evangelist preaching against the wickedness of prejudice. A forceful and dynamic speaker on the subject of women's suffrage and the abolition of slavery, Sojourner Truth delivered this passionate speech in her adopted hometown of Battle Creek, Michigan.

Children, who made your skin white? Was it not God?

Who made mine black? Was it not the same God?

Am I to blame, therefore, because my skin is black?

Does it not cast a reproach on our Maker to despise a part of His children, because He has been pleased to give them a black skin?

Indeed, children, it does; and your teachers ought to tell you so, and root up, if possible, the great sin of prejudice against color from your minds.

While Sabbath school teachers know of this great sin—and not only do not teach their pupils that it is a sin, but too often indulge in it themselves—can they expect God to bless them or the children?

Does not God love colored children as well as white children?

115

And did not the same Savior die to save the one as well as the other?

If so, white children must know that if they go to Heaven, they must go there without their prejudice against color, for in Heaven black and white are one in the love of Jesus.

Now, children, remember what Sojourner Truth has told you, and thus get rid of your prejudice, and learn to love colored children that you may be all the children of your Father who is in Heaven.

Afterward

Sojourner Truth died on November 26, 1883 and is buried in Battle Creek, Michigan.

Selected Reading

Gilbert, Olive. *Narrative of Sojourner Truth, A Bondswoman of Olden Time.* New York, NY: Oxford University Press. 1991.

Mabee, Carleton, and Susan Mabee Newhouse. *Sojourner Truth: Slave, Prophet, Legend.* New York, NY: New York University Press. 1995.

Painter, Neil I. *Sojourner Truth: A Life, A Symbol.* New York, NY: W.W. Norton. 1996.

Washington, Margaret. *Sojourner Truth's America.* Urbana, IL: University of Illinois Press. 2009.

Henry Ward Beecher
Slavery
October 16, 1863

Abolitionist preacher Henry Ward Beecher was born on June 24, 1813 in Litchfield, Connecticut. A graduate of Amherst College and The Lane Theological Seminary, Beecher ministered to several Presbyterian congregations before becoming pastor, in 1847, of Brooklyn, New York's Plymouth Church. The Reverend Beecher's increasingly militant sermons against slavery, "the national sin," gained him the reputation as the "public voice" of the abolition movement. While his sister, Harriet Beecher Stowe, author of Uncle Tom's Cabin, *was far more famous, Henry Ward Beecher was still a force to be reckoned with. The British Government, while remaining officially neutral during the American Civil War, had great sympathy for the Confederacy. In 1863 Beecher began a series of pro-Union addresses while on vacation there. Beecher spoke in Manchester, Glasgow, and Edinburgh, before arriving in Liverpool, where he was met with posters that proclaimed, "[You] must attend and show by your hearts and hands that the industrious classes in this town are opposed to the bloody War which Abraham Lincoln is now waging against his brother in the South, and the dastardly means he is resorting to in employing such tools as Henry Ward Beecher, a minister of the Gospel." Nevertheless, on the night of October 16, 1883, the Reverend Henry Ward Beecher delivered this famous address in Liverpool's Philharmonic Hall.*

For more than twenty-five years I have been made perfectly familiar with popular assemblies in all parts of my country except the extreme south. There has not for the whole of that time been a single day of my life when it would have been safe for me to go south of Mason and Dixon's line in my own country, and all for one reason: my solemn, earnest, persistent testimony against that which I consider to be the most atrocious thing under the sun—the system of American slavery in a great, free republic. I have passed through that early period when right of free speech was denied to me. Again and again I have attempted to address audiences that, for no other crime than that of free speech, visited me with all manner of contumelious epithets; and now since I have been in England, although I have met with greater kindness and courtesy on the part of most than I deserved, yet, on the other hand, I perceive that the Southern influence prevails to some extent in England. It is my old acquaintance; I understand it perfectly—and I have always held it to be an unfailing truth that where a man had a cause that would bear examination he was perfectly willing to have it spoken about....

The things required for prosperous labor, prosperous manufactures, and prosperous commerce are three. First, liberty; second, liberty; third, liberty.... First, there must be liberty to follow those laws of business which experience has developed, without imposts or restrictions, or governmental intrusions. Business simply wants to be let alone. Then, second, there must be liberty to distribute and exchange products of industry in any market without burdensome tariffs, without imposts, and without vexatious regulations. There must be these two liberties—liberty to create wealth, as the makers of it think best according to the light and experience which business has given them; and then liberty to distribute what they have created without unnecessary vexatious burdens.... The third is the necessity of an intelligent and free race of customers. There must be freedom among producers; there must be freedom among the distributers; there must be freedom among the customers. It may not have occurred to you that it makes any difference what one's customers are; but it does, in all regular and prolonged business. The condition of the customer determine show much he will buy, determines of what sort he will buy. Poor and ignorant people buy little and that of the poorest kind. The richest and the intelligent, having the more means to buy, buy the most, and always buy the best. Here, then, are the three liberties: liberty of the producer, liberty of the distributor, and liberty of the consumer. The first two need no discussion—they have been long, thoroughly, and brilliantly illustrated by the political economists of Great Britain, and by her eminent statesmen; but it seems to me that enough attention has not been directed to the third....

It is a necessity of every manufacturing and commercial people that their customers should be very wealthy and intelligent. Let us put the subject before you in the familiar light of your own local experience. To whom do the tradesmen of Liverpool sell the most goods at the highest profit? To the ignorant and poor, or to the educated and prosperous? The poor man buys simply for his body; he buys food, he buys clothing, he buys fuel, he buys lodging. His rule is to buy the least and the cheapest that he can. He goes to the store as seldom as he can,—he brings away as little as he can—and he buys for the least he can. Poverty is not a misfortune to the poor only who suffer it, but it is more or less a misfortune to all with whom they deal. On the other hand, a man well off—how is it with him? He buys in far greater quantity. He can afford to do it; he has the money to pay for it. He buys in far greater variety, because he seeks to gratify not merely physical wants, but also mental wants. He buys for the satisfaction of sentiment and taste, as well as of sense. He buys silk, wool, flax, cotton; he buys all metals—iron, silver, gold, platinum—in short, he buys for all necessities and of all substances. But that is not all. He buys a better quality of goods. He buys richer silks, finer cottons, higher grained wools. Now, a rich silk means so much skill and care of somebody's that has been expended upon it to make it finer and richer; and so of cotton, and so of wool. That is, the price of the finer goods runs back to the very beginning, and remunerates the workman as well as the merchant. Indeed, the whole laboring community is as much interested and profited as the mere merchant, in this buying and selling of the higher grades in the greater varieties and quantities. The law of price is the skill; and the amount of skill expended in the work is as much for the market as are the goods.… [Both] the workman and the merchant are profited by having purchasers that demand quality, variety, and quantity. Now, if this be so in the town or the city, it can only be so because it is a law. This is the specific development of a general or universal law, and therefore we should expect to find it as true of a nation as of a city like Liverpool. I know it is so, and you know that it is true of all the world; and it is just as important to have customers educated, intelligent, mor-

119

al, and rich, out of Liverpool as it is in Liverpool. They are able to buy; they want variety, they want the very best; and those are the customers you want. That nation is the best customer that is freest, because freedom works prosperity, industry, and wealth. Great Britain, then, aside from moral considerations, has a direct commercial and pecuniary interest in the liberty, civilization, and wealth of every people and every nation on the globe.

You have also an interest in this, because you are a moral and a religious people. You desire it from the highest motives, and godliness is profitable in all things, having the promise of the life that is, as well as of that which is to come; but if there were no hereafter, and if man had no progress in this life, and if there were no question of moral growth at all, it would be worth your while to protect civilization and liberty, merely as a commercial speculation.... Wherever a nation that is crushed, cramped, degraded under despotism, is struggling to be free, you ... all have an interest that that nation should be free. When depressed and backward people demand that they may have a chance to rise ... it is a duty for humanity's sake, it is a duty for the highest moral motives, to sympathize with them; but besides all these there is a material and an interested reason why you should sympathize with them. Pounds and pence join with conscience and with honor in this design.

Now, Great Britain's chief want is—what? They have said that your chief want is cotton. I deny it. Your chief want is consumers. You have got skill, you have got capital, and you have got machinery enough to manufacture goods for the whole population of the globe. You could turn out fourfold as much as you do, if you only had the market to sell in.... Therefore, the doctrine how to make customers is a great deal more important to Great Britain than the doctrine how to raise cotton. It is to that doctrine I ask from you, business men, practical men, men of fact, sagacious Englishmen—to that point I ask a moment's attention.

There are no more continents to be discovered.... There is very little hope of any more demand being created by new fields. If you are to have a better market, there must be some kind of

120

process invented to make the old fields better. Let us look at it, then. You must civilize the world in order to make a better class of purchasers. If you were to press Italy down again under the feet of despotism, Italy, discouraged, could draw but very few supplies from you. But give her liberty, kindle schools throughout her valleys, spur her industry, make treaties with her by which she can exchange her wine, and her oil, and her silk for your manufactured goods; and for every effort that you make in that direction there will come back profit to you by increased traffic with her. If Hungary asks to be an unshackled nation, if by freedom she will rise in virtue and intelligence, then by freedom she will acquire a more multifarious industry, which she will be willing to exchange for your manufactures. Her liberty is to be found— where? You will find it in the Word of God, you will find it in the code of history; but you will also find it in the Price Current; and every free nation, every civilized people—every people that rises from barbarism to industry and intelligence—becomes a better customer.... The savage is a man one story deep; the civilized man is thirty stories deep....

What will be the result if this present struggle shall eventuate in the separation of America, and making the South—a slave territory exclusively—and the North a free territory; what will be the first result? You will lay the foundation for carrying the slave population clear through to the Pacific Ocean. That is the first step. There is not a man who has been a leader of the South any time within these twenty years, that has not had this for a plan. It was for this that Texas was invaded, first by colonists, next by marauders, until it was wrested from Mexico. It was for this that they engaged in the Mexican War itself, by which the vast territory reaching to the Pacific was added to the Union. Never have they for a moment given up the plan of spreading the American institution, as they call it, straight through toward the West, until the slave who has washed his feet in the Atlantic shall be carried to wash them in the Pacific.... If the South become a slave empire, what relation will it have to you as a customer? It would be an empire of twelve millions of people. Of these, eight millions are white and four millions black.

Consider that one-third of the whole are the miserably poor, un-buying blacks. You do not manufacture much for them.... One other third consists of a poor, unskilled, degraded white population; and the remainder one-third, which is a large allowance, we will say, intelligent and rich. Now here are twelve millions of people, and only one-third of them are customers that can afford to buy the kind of goods that you bring to market.... [If] by sympathy or help you establish a slave empire, you sagacious Britons—if you like it better, then, I will leave the adjective out—are busy in favoring the establishment of an empire from ocean to ocean that should have fewest customers and the largest non-buying population....

There are some apparent drawbacks that may suggest themselves. The first is that the interests of England consist in drawing from any country its raw material.... The interest of England is not merely where to buy her cotton, her ores, her wool, her linens, and her flax. When she has put her brains into the cotton, and into the linen and flax, and it becomes the product of her looms, a far more important question is, "What can be done with it?"... [If] you should bring over so much cotton from the slave empire you cannot sell back again to the slave empire. Now, it is said that if the South should be allowed to be separate there will be no tariff, and England can trade with her; but if the South remain the United States, it will be bound by a tariff, and English goods will be excluded from it.... [Let] me tell you that the first tariff ever proposed in America was not only supported, by Southern interests and votes, but was originated by the peculiar structure of Southern society. The first and chief difficulty—after the Union was formed under our present Constitution—the first difficulty that met our fathers was, how to raise taxes to support the Government.... They ... proposed that taxes and representation should be on the basis of five black men counting as three white men. In a short time it was found impossible to raise these taxes in the South, and then they cast about for a better way, and the tariff scheme was submitted. The object was to raise the revenue from the ports instead of from the people. The tariff, therefore, had its origin in Southern weaknesses and necessities, and not in

122

the Northern cities. Daniel Webster's first speech was against it; but after it was carried by Southern votes (which for more than fifty years determined the law of the country), New England accepted it, and saying, "It is the law of the land," conformed her industry to it; and when she had got her capital embarked in mills and machinery, she became in favor of it. But the South, beginning to feel, as she grew stronger, that it was against her interest to continue the system, sought to have the tariff modified, and brought it down; though Henry Clay, a Southern man himself, was the immortal champion of the tariff. All his lifetime he was for a high tariff, till such a tariff could no longer stand; and then he was for moderating the tariffs. And there has not been for the whole of the fifty years a single hour when any tariff could be passed without the South. The opinion of the whole of America was tariff, high tariff. I do not mean that there were none that dissented from that opinion, but it was the popular and prevalent cry. I have lived to see the time when, just before the war broke out, it might be said that the thinking men of America were ready for free trade. There has been a steady progress throughout America for free trade ideas.

.... [In] an argument addressed to a commercial people it was perfectly fair to represent that their commercial and manufacturing interests tallied with their moral sentiments; and as by birth, by blood, by history, by moral feeling, and by everything, Great Britain is connected with the liberty of the world, God has joined interest and conscience, head and heart, so that you ought to be in favor of liberty everywhere....

[Let] me turn to some other nearly connected topics. It is said that the South is fighting for just that independence of which I have been speaking. The South is divided on that subject. There are twelve millions in the South. Four millions of them are asking for their liberty. Eight millions are banded together to prevent it. That is what they asked the world to recognize as a strike for independence. Eight million white men fighting to prevent the liberty of four million black men, challenging the world. You cannot get over the fact. There it is; like iron, you cannot stir it. They

123

went out of the Union because slave property was not recognized in it. There were two ways of reaching slave property in the Union—the one by exerting the direct Federal authority—but they could not do that, for they conceived it to be forbidden. The second was by indirect influence. If you put a candle under a bowl it will burn as long as the fresh air lasts, but it will go out as soon as the oxygen is exhausted; and so, if you put slavery into a state where it cannot get more states, it is only a question of time how long it will live. By limiting slave territory you lay the foundation for the final extinction of slavery. Gardeners say that the reason why crops will not grow in the same ground for a long time together, is that the roots excrete poisoned matter which the plants cannot use, and thus poison the grain. Whether this is true of crops or not, it is certainly true of slavery; for slavery poisons the land on which it grows....

[If] you were to limit slavery, and to say, it shall go so far and no farther, it would be only a question of time when it should die of its own intrinsic weakness and disease. Now, this was the Northern feeling. The North was true to the doctrine of constitutional rights. The North refused, by any Federal action within the states, to violate the compacts of the Constitution, and left local compacts unimpaired; but the North, feeling herself unbound with regard to what we call the territories—free land which has not yet state rights—said there should be no more territory cursed with slavery. With unerring instinct the South said, "The Government administered by Northern men on the principle that there shall be no more slave territory, is a Government fatal to slavery"; and it was on that account that they seceded—and the first step which they took when they assembled at Montgomery was to adopt a constitution. What constitution did they adopt? The same form of constitution which they had just abandoned. What changes did they introduce? A trifling change about the presidential term, making it two years longer; a slight change about some doctrine of legislation, involving no principle whatever, but merely a question of policy. But by the constitution of Montgomery they legalized slavery, and made it the organic law of the land. The very Constitution which they said they could not live under when they

124

left the Union they took again immediately afterwards, only altering it on one point, and that was, making the fundamental law of the land to be slavery.… Slavery is the framework of the South; it is the root and the branch of this conflict with the South. Take away slavery from the South, and she would not differ from us in any respect. There is not a single antagonistic interest. There is no difference of race, no difference of language, no difference of law, no difference of constitution; the only difference between us is that free labor is in the North and slave labor in the South.

But I know that you say you cannot help sympathizing with a gallant people. They are the weaker people, the minority; and you cannot help going with the minority who are struggling for their rights against the majority. Nothing could be more generous when a weak party stands for its own legitimate rights against imperious pride and power than to sympathize with the weak. But who ever yet sympathized with a weak thief because three constables had got hold of him? And yet the one thief in three policemen's hands is the weaker party.… Today the South is the minority in America, and they are fighting for independence! For what? I could wish so much bravery had a better cause, and that so much self-denial had been less deluded; that the poisonous and venomous doctrine of state rights might have been kept aloof; that so many gallant spirits, such as Jackson, might still have lived. The force of these facts, historical and incontrovertible, can not be broken, except by diverting attention by an attack upon the North. It is said that the North is fighting for the Union, and not for emancipation. The North is fighting for the Union, for that ensures emancipation.… [The] motive determines the value; and why are we fighting for the Union? Because whenever shall forget the testimony of our enemies. They have gone off declaring that the Union in the hands of the North was fatal to slavery. There is testimony in court for you.

We are fighting for the Union because we believe that preamble which explains the very reason for which the Union was constituted. I will read it: "We"—not the states—"We, the people of the United States, in order to form a more perfect union, establish justice, assure domestic tranquility, provide for the common defense, promote the general welfare, and secure the blessings of liberty, to ourselves and our posterity, do ordain and establish this Constitution of the United States of America." It is for the sake of that justice, that common welfare, and that liberty for which the national Union was established, that we fight for the Union. Because the South believed that the Union was against slavery, they left it....

Well, next it is said that the North treats the Negro race worse than the South. Now, you see I don't fear any of these disagreeable arguments. I am going to face every one of them. In the first place, I am ashamed to confess that such was the thoughtlessness—such was the stupor of the North—that for a period of twenty-five years she went to sleep, and permitted herself to be drugged and poisoned with the Southern prejudice against black men. The evil was made worse because, when any object whatever has caused anger between political parties, a political animosity arises against that object, no matter how innocent in itself, no matter what were the original influences which excited the quarrel. Thus the colored man has been the football between the two parties in the North, and has suffered accordingly. I confess it to my shame. But I am speaking now on my own ground, for I began twenty-five years ago, with a small party, to combat the unjust dislike of the colored man. Well, I have lived to see a total revolution in the Northern feeling; I stand here to bear solemn witness of that. It is not my opinion; it is my knowledge. Those men who undertook to stand up for the rights of all men—black as well as white—have increased in number; and now what party in the North represents those men that resist the evil prejudices of past years? The Republicans are that party. And who are those men in the North that have oppressed the Negro? They are the Peace Democrats; and the prejudice for which in England you are attempting to punish me is a prejudice raised by men who have opposed me all my life. These pro-slavery Democrats abused the Negro. I defended him, and they mobbed me for doing it. Oh, justice! This is as if a man should commit an assault, maim and wound a neighbor, and, a surgeon being called in, should begin to

126

dress his wounds, and by-and-by a policeman should come and collar the surgeon and haul him off to prison on account of the wounds which he was healing.

.... Let us compare the condition of the Negro in the North and the South, and that will tell the story. By express law the South takes away from the slave all attributes of manhood and calls him "chattel," which is another word for "cattle." No law in any Northern state calls him anything else but a person. The South denies the right of legal permanent marriage to the slave. There is not a state of the North where the marriage of the slave is not as sacred as that of any free white man. Throughout the South, since the slave is not permitted to live in anything but in concubinage, his wife, so called, is taken from him at the will of his master, and there is neither public sentiment nor law that can hinder most dreadful and cruel separations every year in every county and town. There is not a state, county, or town, or school district in the North where, if any man dare to violate the family of the poorest black man, there would not be an indignation that would overwhelm him. In the South, by statutory law, it is a penitentiary offense to teach a black man to read and write. In the North not only are hundreds and thousands of dollars expended of state money in teaching colored people, but they have their own schools, their own academies, their own churches, their own ministers, their own lawyers. In the South, black men are bred, exactly as cattle are bred in the North, for the market and for sale. Such dealing is considered horrible beyond expression in the North. In the South the slave can own nothing by law, but in the single city of New York there are ten million dollars of money belonging to free colored people. In the South no colored man can determine where he will work, nor at what he will work; but in the North—except in the great cities, where we are crowded by foreigners—in any country part the black man may choose his trade and work at it, and is just as much protected by the laws as any white man in the land.... In the South, no matter what injury a colored man may receive, he is not allowed to appear in court, nor to testify against a white man. In every single court of the North a respectable colored man is as good a witness as if his

127

face were white as an angel's robe. I ask any truthful and considerate man, whether, in this contrast, it does not appear that, though faults may yet linger in the North uneradicated, the state of the Negro in the North is not immeasurably better than anywhere in the South? And now, for the first time in the history of America—for the first time in the history of the United States—a colored man has received a commission under the broad seal and signature of the President of the United States. This day, Frederick Douglass, of whom you all have heard here, is an officer of the United States, a commissioner sent down to organize colored regiments on Jefferson Davis' farm in Mississippi.

There is another fact that I wish to allude to—not for the sake of reproach or blame, but by way of claiming your more lenient consideration—and that is, that slavery was entailed upon us by your action. Against the earnest protests of the colonists, the then government of Great Britain—I will concede, not knowing what were the mischiefs—ignorantly, but in point of fact, forced slave traffic on the unwilling colonists.

I was going to ask you, suppose a child is born with hereditary disease; suppose this disease was entailed upon him by parents, who had contracted it by their own misconduct, would it be fair that those parents, who had brought into the world the diseased child, should rail at that child because it was diseased? Would not the child have a right to turn around and say, "Father, it was your fault that I had it, and you ought to be pleased to be patient with my deficiencies."

I do not ask that you should justify slavery in us because it was wrong in you two hundred years ago; but having ignorantly been the means of fixing it upon us, now that we are struggling with mortal struggles to free ourselves from it, we have a right to your tolerance, your patience, and charitable construction.

I am every day asked when this war will end. I wish I could tell you; but remember, slavery is the cause of the war. Slavery has been working for more than one hundred years, and a chronic evil cannot be suddenly cured; and as war is the remedy, you must be patient to have the conflict long enough to cure the inveterate hereditary sore. But of one thing I think I may give you assurance—this war won't end until the cancer of slavery is cut out by the roots....

No man can unveil the future; no man can tell what revolutions are about to break upon the world; no man can tell what destiny belongs to France, nor to any of the European powers; but one thing is certain—that in the exigencies of the future there will be combinations and recombinations, and that those nations that are of the same faith, the same blood, and the same substantial interests, ought not to be alienated from each other, but ought to stand together. I do not say that you ought not to be in the most friendly alliance with France or with Germany; but I do say that your own children, the offspring of England, ought to be nearer to you than any people of strange tongue. If there had been any feelings of bitterness in America, let me tell you that they had been excited, rightly or wrongly, under the impression that Great Britain was going to intervene between us and our own lawful struggle. With the evidence that there is no such intention all bitter feelings will pass away. We do not agree with the recent doctrine of neutrality as a question of law. But it is past, and we are not disposed to raise that question.... And now in the future it is the work of every good man and patriot not to create divisions, but to do the things that will make for peace. On our part it shall be done. On your part it ought to be done; and when, in any of the convulsions that come upon the world, Great Britain finds herself struggling single-handed against the gigantic powers that spread oppression and darkness, there ought to be such cordiality that she can turn and say to her first-born and most illustrious child, "Come!" I will not say that England cannot again, as hitherto, single-handed manage any power—but I will say that England and America together for religion and liberty—are a match for the world....

Afterward

After once hearing Henry Ward Beecher speak, Mark Twain remarked that he had watched Beecher "sawing his arms in the air, howling sarcasms this way and that, discharging rockets of poetry and exploding mines of eloquence, halting now and then to stamp his foot three times in succession to emphasize a point." A parishioner wrote of Beecher, "His acting power was marvelous.... He almost invariably rose, and in the excitement of description or argument acted the entire subject as it struck him." Beecher continued to speak out for social justice until his death.

Henry Ward Beecher died on March 8, 1887 and is buried in Brooklyn, New York.

Selected Reading

Applegate, Debby. *The Most Famous Man in America: The Biography of Henry Ward Beecher.* New York, NY: Doubleday. 1996

Beecher, Henry Ward. *Freedom and War: Discourses on Topics Suggested by the Times.* Boston, MA: Ticknor & Fields. 1863.

Hibben, Paxton. *Henry Ward Beecher: An American Portrait.* New York, NY: The Press of the Readers Club. 1942.

Ryan, Halford Ross. *Henry Ward Beecher: Peripatetic Preacher.* New York, NY: Greenwood Press. 1990.

Abraham Lincoln
The Gettysburg Address
November 19, 1863

At the Battle of Gettysburg, July 1-3, 1863, Union and Confederate forces suffered an estimated 45,000 casualties, including 10,500 dead. The dead of both sides were buried on the battlefield. On November 19, 1863, President Lincoln was invited to say a few appropriate words at the dedication ceremony of the Gettysburg National Cemetery. Lincoln spoke for only three minutes, delivering his landmark Gettysburg Address.

Fourscore and seven years ago, our fathers brought forth on this continent a new nation, conceived in liberty, and dedicated to the proposition that all men are created equal.

Now we are engaged in a great civil war, testing whether that nation, or any nation so conceived and so dedicated, can long endure. We are met on a great battlefield of that war. We have come to dedicate a portion of that field as a final resting place for those who here gave their lives that that nation might live. It is altogether fitting and proper that we should do this.

But, in a larger sense, we cannot dedicate, we cannot consecrate, we can not hallow, this ground. The brave men, living and dead, who struggled here, have consecrated it far above our poor power to add or detract. The world will little note nor long remember what we say here, but it can never forget what they did here. It is for us, the living, rather, to be dedicated here to the unfinished work which they who fought here have thus far so nobly advanced. It is rather for us to be here dedicated to the great task remaining before us—that from these honored dead we take increased devotion to that cause for which they gave the last full measure of devotion, that we here highly resolve that these dead shall not have died in vain, that this nation, under God, shall have a new birth of freedom, and that government of the people, by the people, for the people, shall not perish from the earth.

Afterward

Lincoln's Presidency spanned the Civil War. He was assassinated by John Wilkes Booth in April 1863.

Selected Reading

Harrison, Maureen, and Steve Gilbert, Editors. *Abraham Lincoln: Word for Word.* San Diego, CA: Excellent Books. 1993.

Heidorf, Christian J. *Gettysburg: The One Hundred Twenty-Fifth Anniversary: What They Did Here.* 1990.

Randall, J.G., and Richard N. Current. *Lincoln the President: Last Full Measure.* 1991.

Wills, Garry. *Lincoln at Gettysburg: The Words That Remade America.* 1993.

Frederick Douglass
What The Black Man Wants
January 26, 1865

Frederick Augustus Washington Bailey, the son of a black slave, Harriet Bailey, and an unknown white father, was born in February 1817 on a Maryland plantation. In 1838, he escaped to the North on the Underground Railroad. To protect himself from being returned to slavery under the Fugitive Slave Act, he used the name Frederick Douglass. In 1845 he published his autobiography, "Narrative of the Life of Frederick Douglass, an American Slave, Written by Himself," and with the proceeds he purchased his own freedom for $710.96. Known as "The Voice of the Colored People," Douglass spoke eloquently against slavery on behalf of the American Anti-Slavery Society.

.... What is freedom? It is the right to choose one's own employment. Certainly it means that, if it means anything; and when any individual or combination of individuals undertakes to decide for any man when he shall work, where he shall work, at what he shall work, and for what he shall work, he or they practically reduce him to slavery. He is a slave....

I have had but one idea for the last three years to present to the American people, and the phraseology in which I clothe it is the old abolition phraseology. I am for the "immediate, unconditional, and universal" enfranchisement of the black man, in every state in the Union. Without this, his liberty is a mockery; without this, you might as well almost retain the old name of slavery for his condition; for in fact, if he is not the slave of the individual master, he is the slave of society, and holds his liberty as a privilege, not as a right. He is at the mercy of the mob, and has no means of protecting himself.

It may be objected, however, that this pressing of the Negro's right to suffrage is premature. Let us have slavery abolished, it may be said, let us have labor organized, and then, in the natural course of events, the right of suffrage will be extended to the Negro. I do not agree with this. The constitution of the human mind is such that, if it once disregards the conviction forced upon it by a revelation of truth, it requires the exercise of a higher power to produce the same conviction afterwards. The American people are now in tears. The Shenandoah has run blood—the best blood of the North. All around Richmond, the blood of New England and of the North has been shed—of your sons, your brothers, and your fathers. We all feel, in the existence of this Rebellion, that judgments terrible, widespread, far-reaching, overwhelming, are abroad in the land; and we feel, in view of these judgments, just now, a disposition to learn righteousness. This is the hour. Our streets are in mourning, tears are falling at every fireside, and under the chastisement of this Rebellion we have almost come up to the point of conceding this great, this all-important right of suffrage. I fear that if we fail to do it now, if abolitionists fail to press it now, we may not see, for centuries to come, the same disposition that exists at this moment. Hence, I say, now is the time to press this right.

It may be asked, "Why do you want it? Some men have got along very well without it. Women have not this right." Shall we justify one wrong by another? This is the sufficient answer. Shall we at this moment justify the deprivation of the Negro of the right to vote, because someone else is deprived of that privilege? I hold that women, as well as men, have the right to vote, and my heart and voice go with the movement to extend suffrage to woman; but that question rests upon another basis than which our right rests. We may be asked, I say, why we want it. I will tell you why we want it. We want it because it is our right, first of all. No class of men can, without insulting their own nature, be content with any deprivation of their rights. We want it again, as a means for educating our race. Men are so constituted that they derive their conviction of their own possibilities largely by the estimate formed of them by others. If nothing is expected of a people, that people will find it difficult to contradict that expectation. By depriving us of suffrage, you affirm our incapacity to form an intelligent judgment respecting public men and public measures; you declare before the world that we are unfit to exercise the elective

134

franchise, and by this means lead us to undervalue ourselves, to put a low estimate upon ourselves, and to feel that we have no possibilities like other men. Again, I want the elective franchise, for one, as a colored man, because ours is a peculiar government, based upon a peculiar idea, and that idea is universal suffrage. If I were in a monarchial government, or an autocratic or aristocratic government, where the few bore rule and the many were subject, there would be no special stigma resting upon me, because I did not exercise the elective franchise. It would do me no great violence. Mingling with the mass I should partake of the strength of the mass; I should be supported by the mass, and I should have the same incentives to endeavor with the mass of my fellow men; it would be no particular burden, no particular deprivation; but here, where universal suffrage is the rule, where that is the fundamental idea of the Government, to rule us out is to make us an exception, to brand us with the stigma of inferiority, and to invite to our heads the missiles of those about us; therefore, I want the franchise for the black man.

There are, however, other reasons, not derived from any consideration merely of our rights, but arising out of the conditions of the South, and of the country, ... considerations which must arrest the attention of statesmen. I believe that when the tall heads of this Rebellion shall have been swept down, as they will be swept down, when the Davises and Toombses and Stephenses, and others who are leading this Rebellion shall have been blotted out, there will be this rank undergrowth of treason, to which reference has been made, growing up there, and interfering with, and thwarting the quiet operation of the Federal Government in those states. You will see those traitors, handing down, from sire to son, the same malignant spirit which they have manifested and which they are now exhibiting, with malicious hearts, broad blades, and bloody hands in the field, against our sons and brothers. That spirit will still remain; and whoever sees the Federal Government extended over those Southern states will see that Government in a strange land, and not only in a strange land, but in an enemy's land. A postmaster of the United States in the South will find himself surrounded by a hostile spirit; a collector in a Southern port will find himself surrounded by a hostile spirit; a United States marshal or United States judge will be surrounded there by a hostile element. That enmity will not die out in a year, will not die out in an age.... They will endeavor to circumvent, they will endeavor to destroy, the peaceful operation of this Government. Now, where will you find the strength to counterbalance this spirit, if you do not find it in the Negroes of the South? They are your friends, and have always been your friends. They were your friends even when the Government did not regard them as such. They comprehended the genius of this war before you did. It is a significant fact, it is a marvelous fact, it seems almost to imply a direct interposition of Providence, that this war, which began in the interest of slavery on both sides, bids fair to end in the interest of liberty on both sides. It was begun, I say, in the interest of slavery on both sides. The South was fighting to take slavery out of the Union, and the North was fighting to keep it in the Union; the South fighting to get it beyond the limits of the United States Constitution, and the North fighting to retain it within those limits; the South fighting for new guarantees, and the North fighting for the old guarantees—both despising the Negro, both insulting the Negro. Yet, the Negro, apparently endowed with wisdom from on high, saw more clearly the end from the beginning than we did. When Seward said the status of no man in the country would be changed by the war, the Negro did not believe him. When our generals sent their underlings in shoulder straps to hunt the flying Negro back from our lines into the jaws of slavery, from which he had escaped, the Negroes thought that a mistake had been made, and that the intentions of the Government had not been rightly understood by our officers in shoulder straps, and they continued to come into our lines, threading their way through bogs and fens, over briers and thorns, fording streams, swimming rivers, bringing us tidings as to the safe path to march, and pointing out the dangers that threatened us. They are our only friends in the South, and we should be true to them in this their trial hour, and see to it that they have the elective franchise.

I know that we are inferior to you in some things—virtually inferior. We walk about you like dwarfs among giants. Our heads are scarcely seen above the great sea of humanity. The Germans are superior to us; the Irish are superior to us; the Yankees are superior to us; they can do what we cannot, that is, what we have not hitherto been allowed to do. But while I make this admission, I utterly deny that we are originally, or naturally, or practically, or in any way, or in any important sense, inferior to anybody on this globe. This charge of inferiority is an old dodge. It has been made available for oppression on many occasions. It is only about six centuries since the blue-eyed and fair-haired Anglo-Saxons were considered inferior by the haughty Normans, who once trampled upon them. If you read the history of the Norman Conquest, you will find that this proud Anglo-Saxon was once looked upon as of coarser clay than his Norman master, and might be found in the highways and byways of Old England laboring with a brass collar on his neck, and the name of his master marked upon it. You were down then! You are up now. I am glad you are up, and I want you to be glad to help us up also.

The story of our inferiority is an old dodge, as I have said; for wherever men oppress their fellows, wherever they enslave them, they will endeavor to find the needed apology for such enslavement and oppression in the character of the people oppressed and enslaved. When we wanted, a few years ago, a slice of Mexico, it was hinted that the Mexicans were an inferior race, that the old Castilian blood had become so weak that it would scarcely run downhill, and that Mexico needed the long, strong and beneficent arm of the Anglo-Saxon care extended over it. We said that it was necessary to its salvation, and a part of the "manifest destiny" of this Republic, to extend our arm over that dilapidated government. So, too, when Russia wanted to take possession of a part of the Ottoman Empire, the Turks were an "inferior race." So, too, when England wants to set the heel of her power more firmly in the quivering heart of old Ireland, the Celts are an "inferior race." So, too, the Negro, when he is to be robbed of any right which is justly his, is an "inferior man." It is said that we are ignorant; I admit it. But if we know enough to be hung, we know

137

enough to vote. If the Negro knows enough to pay taxes to support the government, he knows enough to vote; taxation and representation should go together. If he knows enough to shoulder a musket and fight for the flag, fight for the government, he knows enough to vote. If he knows as much when he is sober as an Irishman knows when drunk, he knows enough to vote, on good American principles.

But I was saying that you needed a counterpoise in the persons of the slaves to the enmity that would exist at the South after the Rebellion is put down. I hold that the American people are bound, not only in self-defense, to extend this right to the freedmen of the South, but they are bound by their love of country, and by all their regard for the future safety of those Southern states, to do this—to do it as a measure essential to the preservation of peace there. But I will not dwell upon this. I put it to the American sense of honor. The honor of a nation is an important thing. It is said in the Scriptures, "What doth it profit a man if he gain the whole world, and lose his own soul?" It may be said, also—What doth it profit a nation if it gain the whole world, but lose its honor? I hold that the American government has taken upon itself a solemn obligation of honor, to see that this war—let it be long or short, let it cost much or let it cost little—that this war shall not cease until every freedman at the South has the right to vote. It has bound itself to it. What have you asked the black men of the South, the black men of the whole country to do? Why, you have asked them to incur the enmity of their masters, in order to befriend you and to befriend this Government. You have asked us to call down, not only upon ourselves, but upon our children's children, the deadly hate of the entire Southern people. You have called upon us to turn our backs upon our masters, to abandon their cause and espouse yours, to turn against the South and in favor of the North, to shoot down the Confederacy and uphold the flag—the American flag. You have called upon us to expose ourselves to all the subtle machinations of their malignity for all time. And now, what do you propose to do when you come to make peace? To reward your enemies, and trample in the dust your friends? Do you intend to sacrifice the

138

very men who have come to the rescue of your banner in the South, and incurred the lasting displeasure of their masters thereby? Do you intend to sacrifice them and reward your enemies? Do you mean to give your enemies the right to vote, and take it away from your friends? Is that wise policy? Is that honorable? Could American honor withstand such a blow? I do not believe you will do it. I think you will see to it that we have the right to vote. There is something too mean in looking upon the Negro, when you are in trouble, as a citizen, and when you are free from trouble, as an alien. When this nation was in trouble, in its early struggles, it looked upon the Negro as a citizen. In 1776 he was a citizen. At the time of the formation of the Constitution the Negro had the right to vote in eleven states out of the old thirteen. In your trouble you have made us citizens. In 1812 General Jackson addressed us as citizens—"fellow citizens." He wanted us to fight. We were citizens then! And now, when you come to frame a conscription bill, the Negro is a citizen again. He has been a citizen just three times in the history of this government, and it has always been in time of trouble. In time of trouble we are citizens. Shall we be citizens in war, and aliens in peace? Would that be just?

I ask my friends who are apologizing for not insisting upon this right, where can the black man look, in this country, for the assertion of his right, if he may not look to the Massachusetts Anti-Slavery Society? Where under the whole heavens can he look for sympathy, in asserting this right, if he may not look to this platform? Have you lifted us up to a certain height to see that we are men, and then are any disposed to leave us there, without seeing that we are put in possession of all our rights? We look naturally to this platform for the assertion of all our rights, and for this one especially. I understand the anti-slavery societies of this country to be based on two principles—first, the freedom of the blacks of this country; and second, the elevation of them. Let me not be misunderstood here. I am not asking for sympathy at the hands of abolitionists, sympathy at the hands of any. I think the American people are disposed often to be generous rather than just. I look over this country at the present time, and I see Educational

Societies, Sanitary Commissions, Freedmen's Associations, and the like—all very good—but in regard to the colored people there is always more that is benevolent, I perceive, than just, manifested towards us. What I ask for the Negro is not benevolence, not pity, not sympathy, but simply justice. The American people have always been anxious to know what they shall do with us.... Everybody has asked the question, and they learned to ask it early of the abolitionists, "What shall we do with the Negro?" I have had but one answer from the beginning. Do nothing with us! Your doing with us has already played the mischief with us. Do nothing with us! If the apples will not remain on the tree of their own strength, if they are worm-eaten at the core, if they are early ripe and disposed to fall, let them fall! I am not for tying or fastening them on the tree in any way, except by nature's plan, and if they will not stay there, let them fall. And if the Negro cannot stand on his own legs, let him fall also. All I ask is, give him a chance to stand on his own legs! Let him alone! If you see him on his way to school, let him alone, don't disturb him! If you see him going to the dinner table at a hotel, let him go! If you see him going to the ballot box, let him alone, don't disturb him! If you see him going into a workshop, just let him alone; your interference is doing him a positive injury.... Let him fall if he cannot stand alone! If the Negro cannot live by the line of eternal justice, ... the fault will not be yours, it will be his who made the Negro, and established that line for his government. Let him live or die by that. If you will only untie his hands, and give him a chance, I think he will live. He will work as readily for himself as the white man. A great many delusions have been swept away by this war. One was that the Negro would not work; he has proved his ability to work. Another was that the Negro would not fight, that he possessed only the most sheepish attributes of humanity, was a perfect lamb, or an "Uncle Tom," disposed to take off his coat whenever required, fold his hands, and be whipped by anybody who wanted to whip him. But the war has proved that there is a great deal of human nature in the Negro, and that "he will fight," as Mr. Quincy, our President, said, in earlier days than these, "when there is reasonable probability of his whipping anybody."

Afterward

Frederick Douglass died on February 20, 1895.

Selected Reading

Foner, Philip S. *Frederick Douglass: A Biography.* New York, NY: Citadel Press. 1964.

Thompson, Julius E., James L. Conyers, Jr., and Nancy J. Dawson, Editors. *The Frederick Douglass Encyclopedia.* Santa Barbara, CA: Greenwood Press. 2010.

Quarles, Benjamin. *Black Abolitionists.* New York, NY: Oxford University Press. 1969.

Abraham Lincoln
Second Inaugural Address
March 4, 1865

The American Civil War, which had claimed, North and South, over 600,000 dead, was nearly over when Abraham Lincoln took the Presidential Oath of Office for the second time. In his Second Inaugural Address Lincoln began to lay the groundwork for a reunited Nation: "With malice toward none; with charity for all; with firmness in the right, as God gives us to see the right, let us strive on to finish the work we are in, to bind up the nation's wounds."

At this second appearing to take the oath of the presidential office, there is less occasion for an extended address than there was at the first. Then a statement, somewhat in detail, of a course to be pursued, seemed fitting and proper. Now, at the expiration of four years, during which public declarations have been constantly called forth on every point and phase of the great contest which still absorbs the attention, and engrosses the energies of the nation, little that is new could be presented. The progress of our arms, upon which all else chiefly depends, is as well known to the public as to myself; and it is, I trust, reasonably satisfactory and encouraging to all. With high hope for the future, no prediction in regard to it is ventured.

On the occasion corresponding to this four years ago, all thoughts were anxiously directed to an impending civil war. All dreaded it—all sought to avert it. While the inaugural address was being delivered from this place, devoted altogether to saving the Union without war, insurgent agents were in the city seeking to destroy it without war—seeking to dissolve the Union, and divide effects, by negotiation. Both parties deprecated war; but one of them would make war rather than let the nation survive; and the other would accept war rather than let it perish. And the war came.

One eighth of the whole population were colored slaves, not distributed generally over the Union, but localized in the Southern part of it. These slaves constituted a peculiar and powerful interest. All knew that this interest was, somehow, the cause of the war. To strengthen, perpetuate, and extend this interest was the object for which the insurgents would rend the Union, even by war; while the government claimed no right to do more than to restrict the territorial enlargement of it. Neither party expected for the war, the magnitude, or the duration, which it has already attained. Neither anticipated that the cause of the conflict might cease with, or even before, the conflict itself should cease. Each looked for an easier triumph, and a result less fundamental and astounding. Both read the same bible, and pray to the same God; and each invokes His aid against the other. It may seem strange that any men should dare to ask a just God's assistance in wringing their bread from the sweat of other men's faces; but let us judge not that we be not judged. The prayers of both could not be answered; that of neither has been answered fully. The Almighty has his own purposes. "Woe unto the world because of offenses! for it must needs be that offenses come; but woe to that man by whom the offense cometh!" If we shall suppose that American slavery is one of those offenses which, in the providence of God, must needs come, but which, having continued through His appointed time, He now wills to remove, and that He gives to both North and South this terrible war as the woe due to those by whom the offense came, shall we discern therein any departure from those divine attributes which the believers in a Living God always ascribe to Him? Fondly do we hope—fervently do we pray—that this mighty scourge of war may speedily pass away. Yet, if God wills that it continue, until all the wealth piled by the bond-man's two hundred and fifty years of unrequited toil shall be sunk, and until every drop of blood drawn with the lash shall be paid by another drawn with the sword, as was said three thousand years ago, so still it must be said; "the judgments of the Lord are true and righteous altogether."

With malice toward none; with charity for all; with firmness in the right, as God gives us to see the right, let us strive on to finish the work we are in; to bind up the nation's wounds; to care for him who shall have borne the battle, and for his widow, and his orphan—to do all which may achieve and cherish a just and lasting peace, among ourselves, and with all nations.

Afterward

On the night of April 14, 1863, in Washington, D.C.'s Ford's Theater, John Wilkes Booth shot President Abraham Lincoln, who died on April 15, 1863.

Selected Reading

Bishop, Jim. *The Day Lincoln Was Shot.* New York, NY: Harper. 1955.

Harrison, Maureen, and Steve Gilbert, Editors. *Abraham Lincoln: Word for Word.* San Diego, CA: Excellent Books. 1993.

Keneally, Thomas. *Abraham Lincoln.* New York, NY: Upper/Viking. 2003.

Sandburg, Carl. *Abraham Lincoln.* New York, NY: Harcourt, Brace & World. 1939.

Andrew Johnson
Treason Must Be Made Odious
April 4, 1865

"I am the last President of the United States!" said James Buchanan on the eve of the 1860 election. The National Democratic Party had split into two irreconcilable regional factions, the Northern Democrats, who supported Illinois Senator Stephen Douglas, and the Southern Democrats who supported Vice President John C. Breckinridge of Kentucky. Senator Andrew Johnson of Tennessee, a lifelong Democrat, supported the candidacy of Breckinridge but, after the victory of Republican Abraham Lincoln, and the subsequent secession of eleven southern states, Johnson remained loyal to the Federal Government. In the political language of the day Johnson was a "War Democrat." After large parts of Tennessee came back under Union control, Lincoln named Johnson Military Governor of Tennessee with the rank of Brigadier General. He later chose Johnson as his Vice Presidential running mate in 1864 under the banner of the National Union Party. Only the twenty-four northern and western states participated in the 1864 election and the National Union Party ticket of Lincoln-Johnson won by an electoral landslide. As the end of the war drew ever closer, Lincoln proposed a very moderate reconstruction plan, which "radical republicans" thought was far too lenient. Vice President Johnson, siding with Lincoln's opponents, adopted an increasingly radical approach to reconstruction. On the day after Richmond, Virginia fell to the Union Army, Johnson made this speech to a large crowd that had gathered to celebrate in Washington, D.C.'s Willard Hotel.

We are now, my friends, winding up a rebellion—a great effort that has been made by bad men to overthrow the government of the United States, a government founded upon free principles and operated by the best stock of the revolution....

[In the Senate,] I was ... called upon to know what I could do with ... traitors, and I want to repeat my reply here. I said, if we had an Andrew Jackson, he would hang them as high as Haman, but as he is no more and sleeps in his grave in his own beloved state, where traitors and treason have never insulted his tomb and the very earth that covers his remains, humble as I am, when you ask me what I would do, my reply is I would arrest them; I would convict them; and I would hang them.... All that I have—life, limb, and property—have been put at the disposal of the country in this great struggle. I have been in the field, I have been everywhere where this great rebellion was. I have pursued it until I believe I can now see its termination.

Since the world began, there never has been a rebellion of such gigantic proportions, so infamous in character, so diabolical in motive, so entirely disregardful of the laws of civilized war. It has introduced the most savage model of warfare ever practiced upon the earth. I will repeat here a remark for which I have been in no small degree censured. What is it, allow me to ask, that has sustained the nation in this great struggle? The cry has been, you know, that our Government was not strong enough for a time of rebellion—that in such a time she would have to contend against internal weakness as well as internal foes. We have now given the world evidence that each is not the fact; and when the rebellion shall have been crushed out and the nation shall once again have settled down in peace, our Government will rest upon a more enduring basis than ever before. But, my friends, in what has the great strength of the government consisted? Has it been in one in power? Has it been in some autocrat or in some one man who held absolute government? No!

I thank God I have it in my power to promise that the government has derived its strength from the American people. They have issued the edict; they have exercised the power that has resulted in the overthrow of the rebellion and there is not another government upon the face of the earth that could have withstood the shock.

We now congratulate ourselves that we possess the strongest, the freest, and the best government the world over saw. Thank God that we have lived through this trial and that looking in your intelligent faces here today I can announce to you the great fact that Petersburg, the outpost to the strong citadel, has been occupied by our brave and gallant officers and our untiring invincible soldiers. And not content with that, they have captured the citadel itself, the stronghold of traitors. Richmond is ours and is now occupied by the forces of the United States! Her gates have been entered and the glorious stars and stripes, the emblem of Union, of power, and of supremacy, now float over the enemy's capitol! In the language of another, let that old flag rise higher, until it meets the sun in his coming, and let the parting day linger to play upon its ample folds. It is the flag of your country; it is your flag; it is my flag; and it bids defiance to all the nations of the earth and to the encroachments of all the powers combined. It is not my intention to make any imprudent remarks or allusions, but the hour will come when those nations that exhibited toward us such insolence and improper interference in the midst of adversity and as they supposed of our weakness will learn that this is a government of the people, possessing power enough to make itself felt and respected.

In the midst of our rejoicing we must not forget to drop a tear for those gallant fellows who have shed their blood that their government might triumph. We cannot forget them when we view the man-bloody battlefields of the war, the new-made graves [of] our maimed friends and relatives who have left their limbs, as it were, on the enemy's soil, and others who have been consigned to their long narrow houses with no winding sheet save their blankets saturated with their blood.

One word more and I have done. It is this—I am in favor of leniency; but in my opinion evildoers should be punished. Treason is the highest crime known in the catalog of crimes, and for him that is guilty of it—for him that is willing to lift his impious hand against the authority of the nation—I would say death is too easy a punishment. My notion is that treason must be made odious— that traitors must be impoverished, their social power broken though—they must be made to feel the penalty of their crime. You, my friends, have traitors in your very midst and treason needs rebuke and punishment here as well as elsewhere. It is not the men in the field who are the greatest traitors. It is the men who have encouraged them to imperil their lives while they themselves have remained at home at expending their means and exerting all their power to overthrow the government.

Hence I say this—the halter to intelligent, influential traitors! But to the honest boy, to the deluded man who has been deceived into the rebel ranks, I would extend leniency. I would say, return to your allegiance, renew your support to the government, and become a good citizen. But the leaders I would hang. I hold too that wealthy traitors should be made to renumerate those men who have suffered as a consequence of their crime—Union men who have lost their property, who have been driven from their homes, beggars and wanderers among strangers.

It is well to talk about these things here today in addressing the well-informed persons who compose this audience. You can to a very great extent aid in molding public opinion and in giving it a proper direction. Let us commence the work. We have put down these traitors in arms. Let us put them down in law, in public judgment, and in the morals of the world.

Afterward

Vice President Andrew Johnson reiterated what he had said in this speech personally to President Lincoln at their last meeting in the White House on April 14, 1865, just hours before Lincoln's death. As President, Andrew Johnson moderated his views on reconstruction, quickly running afoul of his former radical republican allies. In a bitter struggle for control of the reconstruction of the South, Johnson was impeached by the House of Representatives and, by a single vote in the Senate, escaped removal from office. Johnson failed in his bid to win the Democratic Party's nomination for re-election in 1868 and retired to Tennessee.

Andrew Johnson died on July 31, 1875 and is buried in Greenville, Tennessee.

Selected Reading

Castel, Albert. *The Presidency of Andrew Johnson.* Lawrence, KS: Regents Press of Kansas. 1979.

Hearn, Chester G. *The Impeachment of Andrew Johnson.* Jefferson, NC: McFarland & Co. 2000.

Winston, Robert W. *Andrew Johnson, Plebian and Patriot.* New York, NY: AMS Press. 1970.

Ralph Waldo Emerson
The Death of Abraham Lincoln
April 19, 1865

Ralph Waldo Emerson, the preeminent scholar of his time, was born on May 25, 1803 in Boston, Massachusetts. A graduate of Harvard College, Emerson became a writer, editor, and lecturer. Having seen for himself the effect of slavery while traveling in the South, he wrote, "I think we must get rid of slavery, or we must get rid of freedom.... If you put a chain around the neck of a slave, the other end fastens itself around your own." *Emerson made several attacks on slavery, including a speech on May 3, 1851 in Concord, Massachusetts where, taking up the theme of resistance to injustice, he said of the Fugitive Slave Law,* "An immoral law makes it a man's duty to break it, at every hazard. For virtue is the very self of every man." *On January 31, 1862 Emerson lectured in Washington, DC, demanding immediate emancipation of all slaves. The next day Emerson was invited to the White House to discuss his opinions on emancipation with President Lincoln. Lincoln's Emancipation Proclamation was issued a year later. Upon the death of President Lincoln, Ralph Waldo Emerson delivered this famous eulogy.*

We meet under the gloom of a calamity which darkens down over the minds of good men in all civilized society, as the fearful tidings travel over sea, over land, from country to country, like the shadow of an uncalculated eclipse over the planet. Old as history is, and manifold as are, its tragedies, I doubt if any death has caused so much pain to mankind as this has caused, or will cause, on its announcement—and this not so much because nations are, by modern arts brought so closely together, as because of the mysterious hopes and fears which, in the present day, are connected with the name and institutions of America.

In this country, on Saturday, every one was struck dumb, and saw, at first, only deep below deep, as he meditated on the ghastly blow. And, perhaps, at this hour, when the coffin which contains the dust of the President sets forward on its long march through mourning states, on its way to his home in Illinois, we might well

150

be silent, and suffer the awful voices of the time to thunder to us. Yes, but that first despair was brief—the man was not so to be mourned. He was the most active and hopeful of men; and his work had not perished; but acclamations of praise for the task he had accomplished burst out into a song of triumph, which even tears for his death cannot keep down.

The President stood before us a man of the people. He was thoroughly American, had never crossed the sea, had never been spoiled by English insularity, or French dissipation—a quiet, native, aboriginal man, as an acorn from the oak—no aping of foreigners, no frivolous accomplishments; Kentuckian born, working on a farm, a flatboat man, a captain in the Blackhawk war, a country lawyer, a representative in the rural legislature of Illinois—on such modest foundations the broad structure of his fame was laid. How slowly, and yet by happily prepared steps, he came to his place! All of us remember—it is only a history of five or fix years—the surprise and disappointment of the country at his first nomination at Chicago. Mr. Seward, then in the culmination of his good fame, was the favorite of the Eastern states. And when the new and comparatively unknown name of Lincoln was announced (notwithstanding the report of the acclamations of that convention) we heard the result coldly and sadly. It seemed too rash, on a purely local reputation, to build so grave a trust, in such anxious times; and men naturally talked of the chances in politics as incalculable. But it turned out not to be chance. The profound good opinion which the people of Illinois and of the West had conceived of him, and which they had imparted to their colleagues, that they also might justify themselves to their constituents at home, was not rash, although they did not begin to know the richness of his worth.

A plain man of the people, an extraordinary fortune attended him. Lord Bacon says, Manifest virtues procure reputation; occult ones, fortune. He offered no shining qualities at the first encounter; he did not offend by superiority. He had a face and manner which disarmed suspicion, which inspired confidence, which confirmed good-will. He was a man without vices. He had a strong sense of duty which it was very easy for him to obey. Then he had what farmers call a long head—was excellent in working out the sum for himself—in arguing his case and convincing you fairly and firmly. Then it turned out that he was a great worker, had prodigious faculty of performance, worked easily. A good worker is so rare; everybody has some one disabling quality. In a host of young men that start together and promise so many brilliant leaders for the next age, each fails on trial—one by bad health, one by conceit, or by love of pleasure, or lethargy, or an ugly temper— each has some disqualifying fault that throws him out of the career. But this man was found to the very core, cheerful, persistent, all right for labor, and liked nothing so well.

Then he had a vast good nature, which made him tolerant and accessible to all—fair-minded, leaning to the claim of the petitioner, affable, and not sensible to the affliction which the innumerable visits paid to him, when President, would have brought to any one else. And how this good nature became a noble humanity in many a tragic cafe which the events of the war brought to him everyone will remember, and with what increasing tenderness he dealt when a whole race was on his compassion....

Then his broad good humor, running easily into jocular talk, in which he delighted and in which he excelled, was a rich gift to this wise man. It enabled him to keep his secret, to meet every kind of man and every rank in society, to take off the edge of the severest decisions, to mask his own purpose and sound his companion, and to catch with true instinct the temper of each company he addressed. And, more than all, it is to a man a severe labor, in anxious and exhausting crisis, the natural restorative, good as sleep, and is the protection of the overdriven brain against rancor and insanity.

He is the author of a multitude of good sayings, so disguised as pleasantries that it is certain that they had no reputation at first but as jests; and only later by the acceptance and adoption they find in the mouths of millions, turn out to be the wisdom of the hour. I am sure if this man had ruled in a period of less facility of printing, he would have become mythological in a few years ...

by his fables and proverbs. But the weight and penetration of many passages in his letters, messages, and speeches ... are destined hereafter to wide fame. What pregnant definitions, what unerring common sense, what foresight and ... what humane tone! His brief speech at Gettysburg will not easily be surpassed by words on any recorded occasion....

His occupying the chair of state was a triumph of the good sense of mankind and of the public confidence. This middle-class country has got a middle-class President at last. Yes, in manners, sympathies, but not in powers, for his powers were superior. his mind mastered the problem of the day; and, as the problem grew, so did his comprehension of it. Rarely was man so fitted to the event. In the midst of fears and jealousies, in the Babel of counsels and parties, this man wrought incessantly with all his might and all his honesty, laboring to find what the people wanted, and how to obtain that. It cannot he said there is any exaggeration of his worth. If ever a man was fairly tested he was. There was no lack of resistance, nor of slander, nor of ridicule. The times have allowed no state secrets; the nation has been in such a ferment, such multitudes had to be trusted, that no secret could he kept. Every door was ajar, and we know all that befell.

Then, what an occasion was the whirlwind of the war! Here was place for no holiday magistrate, no fair-weather sailor; the new pilot was hurried to the helm in a tornado. In four years—four years of battle days—his endurance, his fertility of resources, his magnanimity, were sorely tried and never found wanting. There, by his courage, his justice, his even temper, his fertile counsel, his humanity, he stood, an heroic figure in the center of a heroic epoch. He is the true history of the American people in his time. Step by step he walked before them—slow with their slowness, quickening his march by theirs; the true representative of this continent, an entirely public man, father of his country, the pulse of twenty millions throbbing in his heart, the thought of their minds articulated by his tongue.

... [Who] does not see, eyen in this tragedy so recent, how fast the terror and ruin of the massacre are already burning into glory

153

around the victim? Far happier this fate than to have lived to be wished away; to have watched the decay of his own faculties; to have seen … the proverbial ingratitude of statesmen; to have seen mean men preferred. Had he not lived long enough to keep the greatest promise that ever man made to his fellow men—the practical abolition of slavery? He had seen Tennessee, Missouri, and Maryland emancipate their slaves. He had seen Savannah, Charleston, and Richmond surrendered; had seen the main army of the rebellion lay down its arms. He had conquered the public opinion of Canada, England, and France. Only Washington can compare with him in fortune.

And what if it should turn out, in the unfolding of the web, that he had reached the term; that this heroic deliverer could no longer serve us; that the rebellion had touched its natural conclusion, and what remained to be done required new and uncommitted hands—a new spirit born out of the ashes of the war; and that Heaven, wishing to show the world a completed benefactor, shall make him serve his country even more by death than his life. Nations, like kings, are not good by facility and complaisance. The kindness of kings consists in justice and strength. Easy good nature has been the dangerous foible of the Republic, and it was necessary that its enemies should outrage it, and drive us to unwonted firmness, to secure the salvation of this country in the next ages.

…. There is a serene Providence which rules the fate of nations, which makes little account of time, little of one generation or race, makes no account of disasters, conquers alike by what is called defeat or by what is called victory, thrusts aside enemy and obstruction, crushes everything immoral as inhuman, and obtains the ultimate triumph of the best race by the sacrifice of everything which resists the moral laws of the world. It makes its own instruments, creates the man for the time, trains him in poverty, inspires his genius, and arms him for his task. It has given every race its own talent, and ordains that only that race which combines perfectly with the virtues of all shall endure.

154

Afterward

On January 1, 1863, during the celebration of the Emancipation Proclamation becoming law, Emerson read his poem, The Boston Hymn, *to a gathering at the Boston Music Hall. It reads in part:*

> *"Break your bonds and masterships,*
> *And I unchain the slave:*
> *Free be his heart and hand henceforth,*
> *As wind and wandering wave."*

Ralph Waldo Emerson died on April 27, 1882 and is buried in Concord, Massachusetts.

Selected Reading

Allen, Gay Wilson. *Waldo Emerson: A Biography.* New York, NY: Viking Press. 1981.

Field, Peter S. *Ralph Waldo Emerson: The Making of a Democratic Intellectual.* Lanham, MD: Rowman & Littlefield. 2002.

Gougeon, Len, and Joel Myerson, Editors. *Emerson's Antislavery Writings.* New Haven, CT: Yale University Press. 1995.

Robinson, David M., Editor. *The Political Emerson: Essential Writings on Politics and Social Reform.* Boston, MA: Beacon Press. 2004.

ALSO AVAILABLE FROM EXCELLENT BOOKS

LANDMARK DECISIONS
OF THE UNITED STATES SUPREME COURT

Our critically-acclaimed series, containing the most significant U.S. Supreme Court decisions, edited into plain non-legal English for the general reader. Topics include:

Volume I: school desegregation, obscenity, school prayer, fair trials, sexual privacy, censorship, abortion, affirmative action, book banning, and flag burning.

Volume II: slavery, women's suffrage, Japanese-American concentration camps, bible reading in the public schools, the book banned in Boston, rights of the accused, the death penalty, homosexuality, offensive speech, and the right to die.

Volume III: executive privilege, clear and present danger, forced sterilization, mob justice, the Pledge Of Allegiance, illegal search and seizure, interracial marriage, monkey trials, sexual harassment, and separation of church and state.

Volume IV: federal supremacy, the Trail of Tears, Lincoln's suspension of habeas corpus, separate but equal, trust busting, child labor, the atomic spies, libel, conscientious objection, and hate crimes.

Volume V: the slave ship cases, religious liberty, treason, military justice, marijuana, birth control, baseball, equal pay for equal work, child abuse, and the "Son of Sam" law.

Volume VI: the Aaron Burr conspiracy, the Dartmouth College case, women's work, the right to bear arms, the "sick chicken" case, the law of war, un-American activities, one person/one vote, the Presidential line item veto, and the right to die.

Volume VII: violence against women, partial birth abortions, the gay scout master, the contested Presidential election, executing the mentally retarded, internet pornography, the al Qaeda cases, medical marijuana, the Ten Commandments cases, affirmative action, sodomy, and private property rights.

📖 EXCELLENT BOOKS ORDER FORM 📖
(Please xerox this form so it will be available to other readers.)

Please send the following books:
___ Landmark Decisions of the U.S. Supreme Court I
___ Landmark Decisions of the U.S. Supreme Court II
___ Landmark Decisions of the U.S. Supreme Court III
___ Landmark Decisions of the U.S. Supreme Court IV
___ Landmark Decisions of the U.S. Supreme Court V
___ Landmark Decisions of the U.S. Supreme Court VI
___ Landmark Decisions of the U.S. Supreme Court VII
___ Barack Obama: Speeches on the Road to the White House
___ The Speeches of Ronald Reagan
___ The Speeches of Abraham Lincoln

All Excellent Books are $24.95 each.
Order directly from us for a discount.
Add $2.00 shipping/handling for the first book
and $1.00 each for every other book ordered.

Name: _____

Organization: _____

Address: _____

E-mail: _____ Fax: _____

City: _____ State: _____ Zip: _____

Send your check or purchase order to:
**Excellent Books, Suite 108A-204; 300 Carlsbad Village Drive;
Carlsbad, CA 92008-2999**
Phone: **760-305-9835**; Fax: **831-618-4698**
E-mail: **books@excellentbooks.com**
or visit our website at www.excellentbooks.com